new fashion illustration

martin dawber

B T BATSFORD

For four cool cats, Ben, Jerry, Jake and Heidi, and all those students (past and present) who continue to teach me

First published in the United Kingdom in 2005 by
BT Batsford
151 Freston Road
London
W10 6TH

An imprint of Anova Books Company Ltd

DESIGNER: Neil Stevens

ISBN-13 9780713489613
ISBN-10 0 7134 8961 8

A CIP catalogue record for this book is available from the British Library.

10 9 8 7 6 5 4 3 2

Printed and bound in China by SNP Leefung

This book can be ordered direct from the publisher at the website: www.anovabooks.com, or try your local bookshop

Distributed in the United States and Canada by Sterling Publishing Co., 387 Park Avenue South, New York, NY 10016, USA

illustration (front cover)
marc

artist
autumn whitehurst

date
2003

media/techniques
adobe photoshop and illustrator

illustration (back cover)
untitled

artist
frédéric desmots

date
2004

media/techniques
adobe photoshop and illustrator

illustration (opposite)
pale face

artist
anjin

date
2003

media/techniques
adobe photoshop and painter

Contents

Foreword

The last ten years have seen the increasing development of new professional characters in the fashion field. We have seen the transformation of the fashion designer to conceptual art director; someone able to sell more than just clothes, but also a world of fantasies and dreams. This is nothing new; since the very beginning of the fashion industry as we conceive it, the fashion designer's objectives share a close relationship with this world of dreams. The lack of universal trends in an increasingly globalized world opens the gates for freedom and individualism. The illustration process is profoundly affected by this – it is the language used by designers to convey their dreams, messages and fantasies.

The cultural roots of artists are becoming so subtle that it is now difficult for the viewer to distinguish their nationality. The world wide web is creating new, interesting characters in which Turkish, English, Belgian, Italian, Korean or American creators reflect a mixed, individualized culture in which references are part of an increasing melting pot.

The objective of the illustration in contemporary times is more and more concerned with painting characters – in the deep sense of the word. The contamination of modern artistic expression, along with cinema, digital instruments, music, and languages, introduces new borders to the world of fashion illustration that must be overcome. It becomes more and more difficult to distinguish fashion illustration from forms of art, modern stripes or storyboards. A mixture of techniques, combined with personal interpretations of body, silhouette and colour, result in illustrations that offer emotion, a new kind of language, that touches our souls before our brains. This is probably what fashion is required to be nowadays, much more so than yesterday.

Fashion illustration has a significant advantage over any other expression of fashion; from photography to real sketches, it allows the designer to paint his world of reference, in 360 degrees, without constrictions. It is not something merely related to technique, but it is about feelings. Those same feelings that can be read in the images, full of richness and emotions, are as important as predicting future avenues of fashion.

Barbara Trebitsch
Designer and Director of the Master Course in Fashion Design
Domus Academy, Italy

illustration
woman in patterned jacket

artist
jen renninger

date
2002

media/techniques
watercolour, gouache, ink,
graphite, adobe photoshop

Introduction

'Knowledge is limited. Imagination often encircles the world.'
Albert Einstein, 1879–1955

The artistic language of fashion illustration has undergone a radical adjustment within the past two decades, spurred on by the new wave of fashion designers. Their increasingly adventurous drift away from the traditional values of clothes and dress codes has demanded a resurgence in style and execution by today's fashion illustrators. Mirroring these radical developments, today's illustrators have been required to challenge the norm with creative and imaginative representations that act as the barometer to this change. The Barbiesque conventions of long legs, narrow waists and small heads are no longer *de rigueur* or considered appropriate. Currently, fashion illustration remains a creative process now employing art and technology to convey ideas.

Illustration has always been in evidence, in its broadest sense, to document the modes and manners of society in a style that was considered a reflection of its time. From the earliest scratchings on the cave wall, via the legacy of court painting, through to the variety of 20th-century expression, the vernacular of mannered representation of the human figure has always populated our culture. In 1912 the hybrid of fashion illustration *per se* gained ground with the appearance of *Le Gazette du BonTon* in Paris, published by Lucien Vogel – the accepted forerunner of today's fashion magazines. It relied upon printed line drawings that were later individually hand-coloured. The career of many fashion illustration pioneers started with their exposure in *Le Gazette du BonTon*. Georges Lepape, Paul Iribe, Romain de Tirtoff (Erté) and Georges Barbier all featured within its covers (and often on them as well).

In the decades that followed there was increased popular international demand for more fashion-orientated magazines (enter Condé Nast) which, before the later monopoly of the photographic image, increased the opportunity for artists and illustrators in the 1920s and 1930s to continue to provide stylish renditions in response to the latest fashion trends. Such was the attraction of illustrating fashion that notable artists also contributed to the form: Raoul Duffy, Rene Magritte and Sonia Delauney. Although consummate draughtsmen like Carl Erickson (Eric) and Count Renato Zavagli Ricciardelli delle Camminate (René Gruau) valiantly upheld the tradition during the 1940s with their heavily brushed ink and charcoal outlines, by the 1950s illustration was being elbowed out of fashion magazines now returning to full circulation after the war years (barring the few crumbs of advertising space). The following decades progressively saw the advances of an increasingly creative camera lens to report on fashion.

During the 1960s and 1970s only a limited number of exponents of the craft were able to maintain their credibility against the over-saturation of these new wave photographers (Puerto-Rican born Antonio Lopez at *Women's Wear Daily* and the *New York Times* being the obvious 'star' contender) and it seemed that fashion illustration would never again rise above its relegation to the 'health and beauty tips' division within the established glossies.

However, all this was set to change during the 1980s with runway supermodels edged off the designer catwalks and the arrival of a totally new fashion press out to make instant impact. Magazines such as *The Face* and *i-D*, sporting revolutionary art direction by Neville Brody and supersnapper Nick Knight, shook the establishment with their provocative and uncompromising takes upon fashion and design – for these publications the emphasis was on liberation and style out on the street. These were refreshing publishing cocktails that mixed all the elements of a vibrant youth culture into a visual manifesto that catalogued its movers and shakers with a no-holds-barred approach. *Tank* and *Dazed & Confused* took up their mantle and equally paved the way for others, such as *Wallpaper**, to continue to respond creatively to fashion reportage, which has latterly seen increase through designer e-magazines and internet sites.

Today, the hand-tinted fashion plate of the 1900s has evolved into the virtual interface of a plasma screen as illustrators become increasingly fascinated with the potential of computer-aided design, not only as an additional piece of kit, but also as a powerful catalyst for their innovation. These pixel pushers stunningly illustrate fashion by taking advantage of the creative media that has impacted on so much of life in the 21st century.

The test of the past 20 years has prompted new generations of illustrators and artists to pump a transfusion of much-needed new blood into the methods and techniques of their ancestors, to launch their own personal language of fashion illustration. It is no longer acceptable to only capture the new season from a Paris or Italian catwalk: today's fashion illustrator is far more attracted to the evidence on the street, from the people around them. Fashion has now flown away from the ivory tower dictate of the few and originates in the idealism of the individual.

Oscar de la Renta, in an interview in the *New York Times Magazine* in 2002 acknowledged that 'Women dress today to reveal their personalities. They used to reveal the designer's personality. Until the 1970s, women listened to designers. Now women want to do it their own way'.

Two recent key illustrators, Graham Rounthwaite and Jason Brooks, enhanced a stylized representation technique that, although dipping the nod to past masters of the form, turned out to be an entirely new technique in their imaginative hands. The influence of their digital handwriting has spawned the current surfeit of vector overdrive in illustration.

In the current reappraisal, the traditional skills of drawing and painting are now being mixed with contemporary practice and media to appeal to the developed sense of aesthetic sensibilities that today's audience commands. Illustration is once more confirming itself as a prime documenter of fashion and lifestyle. The 'poor man's photography' metaphor is being truly put to shame as software programs and digital photography encourage the methods of the illustrator and photography increasingly becomes more akin to illustration.

Today's illustrators are equally compelled to journey outside the boundaries of convention by the attitudes and dress codes that are fashioned around them, as much as by the unprecedented box of tricks that they have at their fingertips. Just as fashion continues to edge away from apparel towards art and self-expression, so the illustrator of that fashion needs to draw upon all his expertise and skill to articulate this new aesthetic.

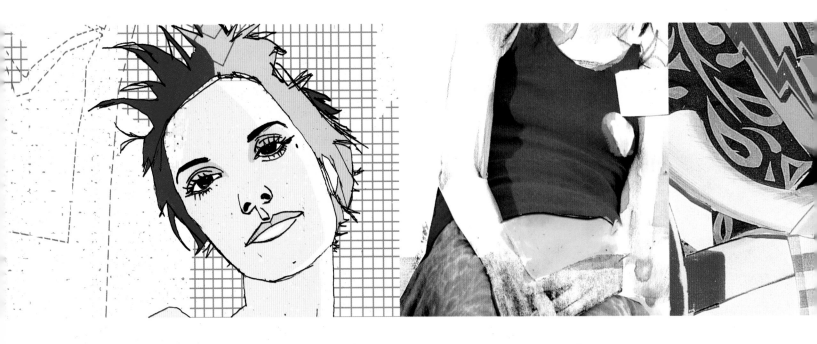

Europe

Patrick Morgan

birthplace London, England
education Kingston University, London, England
inspiration David Hockney, Damien Hirst, Tom Ford, Nick Knight, Paul Smith

Born in London, I had a childhood that was very stimulating, loud and full of adventure. Art was encouraged by my mum, as she felt it kept us quiet, and got the creative juices flowing, using old washing-up bottles, egg cartons and whatever else was available. I started drawing because we were expected to create amazing cards for my nan and granddad every Sunday when they visited, and mine tended to be the most imaginative. This is still a strong tradition today, and my girlfriend still gets one on every visit!

I take inspiration from Jean Michel Basquiat, Francis Bacon, David Hockney, Damien Hirst, Tom Ford, my dad (Patrick Morgan Senior), Nick Knight, Peter Saville and, finally, Paul Smith. Studying illustration at Kingston, I learnt not only how to draw, but how to express ideas through different mediums, and I received a commendation in printmaking. The use of printmaking has helped me to understand the traditional methods of print, which is vital in the advertising and design industry.

Since graduating I have received commissions from clients worldwide. My portfolio includes Levi's, Selfridges, Gordon's Gin, Virgin Airways, 3 mobile, Nars Cosmetics, the *Guardian*, Nike, *Time Out*, Siemens, Nokia, MTV, BBC, Abbey National, British Airways, the Body Shop, Carling Black Label, and numerous editorials.

I also teach fashion illustration at Instituto Marangoni in London, where I encourage students to express their designs through illustration instead of the medium of photography, which has dominated fashion advertising recently – unlike in the 1960s, when artists such as Andy Warhol and Antonio Lopez were pioneers in the use of illustration in the advertising industry.

In contrast with the methods I teach at Marangoni, where the focus is on traditional drawing and coloured renderings, my own style incorporates both old and new techniques. Today, everyone wants to know about Adobe Photoshop and Illustrator software, but these methods do not improve creativity and should only be used as tools to extend ideas.

illustration
nars new york – dirty diane

date
2004

media/techniques
screen printing, adobe
photoshop, pencils

My style always starts in a small sketchbook, jotting down ideas, inspirations and compositions. I take photographs and sketch on location and from still life. I will send a client a rough drawing, answering the brief, to give them an understanding of my thought process. Once I get the thumbs up, I can begin to add some life to the image by scanning different textures, materials, photocopies and photographs. I try to incorporate objects like this all the time, from magazine cuttings to leaf and tree rubbings. Only then do I clean up my images in Adobe Photoshop, by using alpha channels, and make the black outlines totally opaque, mirroring the screen print method. After cleaning up the drawing, I apply depth to the image by using multiple layers, varying in transparency, colour and texture. Even though the process seems easy on the computer, in reality, it is not so simple. The knowledge I gained from screen printing and traditional methods helps me to plan the direction of the illustration more easily.

10

illustration
selfridges annual report

date
2003

media/techniques
pencils, adobe photoshop

illustration
levi's promotion

date
2003

media/techniques
pencils, adobe illustrator, adobe
photoshop

illustration
levi's promotion

date
2003

media/techniques
pencils, adobe illustrator, adobe
photoshop

illustration
nars japan – sexy sandra

date
2004

media/techniques
screen printing, adobe
photoshop, pencils

Erin Petson

birthplace Middlesbrough, England
education John Moores University, Liverpool, England
inspiration Mats Gustafson, François Berthoud, Ruben Alterio, Egon Schiele

I was born in Middlesbrough, in the northeast of England. I graduated from the Liverpool Art School, John Moores University, with a first class honours degree in Graphics. As a child, I was always drawing and painting, and not surprisingly my favourite subject at school was art, especially drawing. Growing up, I was influenced by films – everything from Ridley Scott's *Blade Runner* to Audrey Hepburn in *My Fair Lady*. Looking back, I realize now that it was the costumes that held my attention and was the start of my journey to becoming a fashion illustrator.

Drawing is the most basic form of communication and that's why I like it. You express your ideas and thoughts instantly on a piece of paper. It is personal and emotional; you become very engrossed in it. Fashion illustration is a personal way of visually communicating a style, not unlike the way in which we express ourselves through our clothes. In the last few years there has been a significant revival in illustration and particularly in fashion illustration, which I think is challenging the supremacy of the fashion photograph. It's a very exciting time and I am pleased to be part of it.

My style of illustration has developed through experimentation with different styles and techniques, but also by learning from my mistakes. The process is challenging, as you continually question what you are doing. Is it right? Should I adapt it? Should I start again? It can be frustrating, but it is also very satisfying when you get it right.

I start by taking photographs of my friends, and always try to create dramatic, visually interesting poses, which I know will illustrate well. I then start to draw from my photographs, and sometimes use images from magazines and books to create an original piece of work. I always experiment with ways of working, but initially I work in pencil and ink on paper. I also introduce more collage on top of the drawings. When I have completed my illustrations I scan them into my computer and use Adobe Photoshop and Illustrator to manipulate and layout the image, and play around with the levels of brightness to make the lines more intense. I then use screen printing to build up layers and play around with the scale. I blur or cover the facial features of the models so as not to distract from the clothing. I believe this gives a distinctive edge to my illustrations. My illustrations incorporate abstractions of human form, to highlight and play with contemporary themes of youth, beauty and consumer lifestyles.

illustration
girl with lipstick

date
2004

media/techniques
pencil, ink, screen printing, adobe photoshop, adobe illustrator

Many artists influence me. I've always admired fashion illustrators such as Mats Gustafson, François Berthoud and Ruben Alterio. I like the simplicity of Gustafson's silhouettes and the atmosphere he creates. Berthoud's use of print gives him a unique style. I love the sense of movement you get from the brush strokes in Alterio's designs. The figurative work of the artists R B Kitaj and Egon Schiele has always been an influence in my work, and I also like the abstract drawings of Cy Twombly. Contemporary illustrators such as Marion Deuchars and Aude Van Ryn have also been very influential to me.

illustration
cross girl

date
2004

media/techniques
collage, pen, ink, screen
printing, adobe photoshop,
adobe illustrator

illustration
girl wearing

date
2004

media/techniques
collage, pen, ink, screen
printing, adobe photoshop,
adobe illustrator

Rob Phillips

birthplace Birmingham, England
education Ravensborne College of Design and Communication, London, England
inspiration Peter Saville, Gary Hume, Gustav Klimt, Jenny Saville, Andy Warhol

I grew up in Birmingham, but moved to London to study Fashion at Ravensborne College of Design and Communication. Growing up, I was always drawing, from cartoon characters (always the bad guys) to still life, and eventually turned to fashion and figurative illustration, particularly womenswear design.

As a freelance fashion image-maker, I have worked with numerous publications and have helped designers visualize or characterize their ideas. Magazines are the best way to exhibit my work as I love graphics and text. It really works well with my style, even down to the glossy or trashy paper it's printed on, which adds to the overall finished look.

Often I am drawn to exceptionally graphic artists, such as Peter Saville, Gary Hume and Super Studio. I also love Gustav Klimt, Egon Schiele and Jenny Saville for the quality and sensitivity of their work. Andy Warhol must be one of my biggest inspirations.

Illustration takes fashion further. You can draw any outfit or situation, and create positions that are not really possible but that look fabulous and uncannily real. I rarely offer depth in my work; there is little, if any, meaning. It's not what I am about. My work is of a moment, what's going on in my head, images or words that epitomize a style or story. There's movement, styling, maybe a scenario, but little facial emotion. It is the pose or silhouette that embodies a feeling.

Images begin with simple sketches, doodles and page plans. The initial picture in my head is never what I ultimately produce, but it makes for instant inspiration and sourcing of colours and fabrics. I find bits of patterns or shades of colour and start thinking about their placement on the sketch. That then usually adds a new feeling and changes the direction of the mood or style. Sometimes I build up collage on pencil lines, or just use cuttings and tear sheets.

illustration (opposite)
boys and cars

date
2004

media/techniques
decoupage

illustration (next page)
petrol station

date
2004

media/techniques
decoupage

I have also always been influenced by textiles, especially print and dye methods. I used a ball of yarn that had fantastic tones of colour to do something practical and messy rather than simple drawings. I dipped yarn into a variety of dyes to create a spectrum of vivid colours and create wonderful figures and clothing from the result. I have also worked with chamois leather and other fabrics to create beautiful, abstract, paisley-embossed prints in delicious shades of camel, chocolate and tangerine. The luxury of the cloth inspired me to draw ladies with plenty of curves and swirls, kind of noveau and influenced by the style of Alphonse Mucha. The best lesson I ever learnt was to simply let go, don't try to achieve what's in your head, try to develop what is on the paper.

There's been much interest in what I do, especially in the hand-rendered pieces – which is perfect because that's how I love to work. Freehand illustration is a dying medium. Computers have taken over but never quite get that incidental quality. Traditional methods are great for me: drawing, cutting, stencils, painting, photocopying. I love these processes because they add character and accidental, yet aesthetically pleasing, elements.

Rob Phillips

illustration
dips an' strands

date
2004

media/techniques
ink, dye, yarn, decoupage

illustration
easy girl

date
2004

media/techniques
stencils, pencils

Flo H

birthplace London, England
education Royal College of Art, London, England
inspiration Philip Guston, Pablo Picasso, Jackson Pollock, Marcel Duchamp

I was born and bred in London. I studied at the Surrey Institute of Art and Design and the Royal College of Art, London.

I tend to go with ideas that are enjoyable, interesting and thought-provoking. I make a mess at all times and, wherever I am, I will often be surrounded by bits of paper, newspaper clippings, old books and photographs, scalpels, spray mount and hundreds of pencils, pastels and paints. To work this way is my release, a method of personal expression. The rules go out of the window and my mind is free to play.

The combination of my hand, eye and camera supports my love of image making, seeing the world through a new set of tools and constantly moving through the flow of it. Someone told me on my travels: 'You draw in the craziest of ways, it is like you always want to start something completely different on the same page without even moving from it.' Perhaps this is not the correct way of drawing an object or a figure – but is there a really correct way?

I work for the love of it; I don't believe there is a point otherwise. I try to focus on my own sense of creating rather than labelling what I do. I like to have challenges, love to work on briefs and enjoy the influences in my life and the amazing artwork I research from all over the world. I generally work from very simple sketches that I do while I am out of the studio. They enable me to get a feeling for what I am looking at rather than trying to recall a certain situation or person. From an initial idea and sketch, I would normally turn to my computer to consider ways of manipulating colours, shapes and forms. I make simple collages of textured paper, paint, inks and newsprints. This method has gradually developed as I have more trust in my hand's eye and now enjoy a more loosely formed approach to creating an image. I like to create work using layers and not worry too much about the aesthetic of the piece as long as I am communicating a message or feeling. Most importantly, I record my experiences through my drawings, photographs and film-work; capturing people in their natural habitats and constantly observing the light, the sound and the touch of the often-troubled world in which we live.

illustration
tracey in armarni

date
2003

media/techniques
collage

As for the artists that interest me, the list is endless, from Chris Ofili, Olafur Eliasson, Zarina Bhimji, Michael Landy, and Jake and Dinos Chapman to Philip Guston, Pablo Picasso, Jackson Pollock, Marcel Duchamp, Gary Taxali and a favourite Vietnamese artist, Le Thanh Thu. I could go on. I like to research contemporary artists from all corners of the globe and, in a couple of years, I hope to travel again to experience the work first hand. Until that time, I believe it is important to have an open mind, to grasp opportunities, not to regret, to accept that failures and rewards will come and go, and that to wonder far from the straight path means to explore something new.

illustration
from hoi ann

date
2004

media/techniques
collage

illustration
no place i know

date
2004

media/techniques
collage

illustration
phenh pen at last

date
2004

media/techniques
collage

illustration
local

date
2004

media/techniques
collage

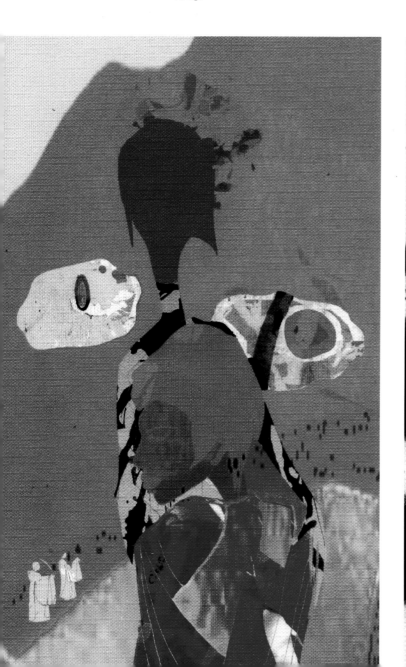

Annette-Marie Pearcy

birthplace London, England
education University of Westminster, London, England
inspiration Sarah Jane Szikora, Beryl Cook, Fernando Botero, Eva Hannah

I adore the art of illustration. It is a force and a passion that rages within me and it is the way I communicate with the world. The youngest of four, my illustrations began at two years old; my canvas then was my bedroom walls, much to my parents' dismay. At school, I would spend hours creating pictures to accompany homework. I graduated from the University of Westminster in London with a degree in illustration.

Over the years I have developed my own distinctive style, which combines collage with photography, and which I have adapted and nurtured throughout my career as a freelance illustrator. My style focuses on producing characters, often female, and created thematically. They often appear quirky and candid in their finished format, the result of my take or observations of life. I like to think of the images as a social commentary or a 'slice of life'. They begin their lives as rough sketches that have sprung from various inspirations, from a simple conversation between friends to simply a look or pose of a particular person in an ordinary setting. Each image is a cocktail of my favourite things; I approach an illustration like a fashion shoot where I take the role of make-up artist, stylist and photographer, working in a very precise, organized way.

Once the initial sketch is complete, I begin to build the image from scratch with materials gleaned from photographs and magazine cuttings. You could say my work is a kind of recycling process. I currently have a whole library of noses, ears, eyes and outfits, which I have accumulated over the years. I love surrounding myself with these inanimate parts. Then I slowly wield my creative talents to draw these parts together like a jigsaw puzzle and produce a new image that can then take on its own life and personality. The foundations of my figures are the faces, consisting of up to 12 cuttings. They may also be layered and manipulated in the computer depending on the desired expression and position. When the faces are complete the rest of the illustration follows. Hair is built up from various strands, tones and highlights, giving it depth and shape. The creases, folds and movement of photographed fabrics allow me to dress my figures as though they own their clothes. The final artwork is scanned into the computer using Adobe Photoshop, then cleaned and manipulated using layers and filters. The completed image is then set against a manipulated photographic background to create the space in which the character begins to exist.

Working in this way has proved to be very rewarding work for me; my images have been embraced by clients such as Macmillan Education, Toni & Guy, EHS Brann, *Reader's Digest* and *Women's Health* magazine.

illustration
girl's night

date
2003

media/techniques
collage, photography, adobe
photoshop

A variey of artists have been my inspiration: for example, Sarah Jane Szikora, Beryl Cook and the Colombian artist Fernando Botero. I am also a huge fan of Eva Hannah, whom I stumbled across when I visited Sydney. I am drawn to her caricatures that, like my own work, provide a commentary on life. As for my own art … I just want to leave my mark on the world, however big or small that may be.

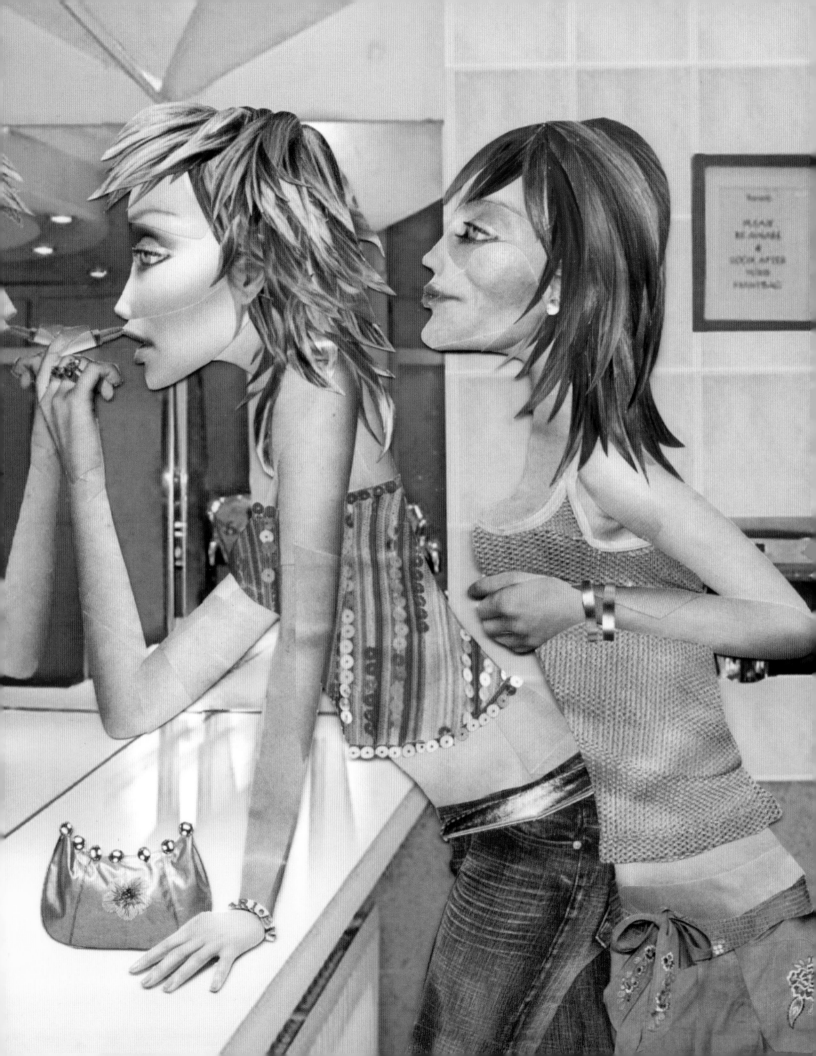

illustration
girlie chat

date
2003

media/techniques
collage, photography, adobe
photoshop

illustration
ladies room

date
2003

media/techniques
collage, photography, adobe
photoshop

illustration (above)
the right bag can make
your outfit

date
2004

media/techniques
collage, photography, adobe
photoshop

illustration (above)
shoe heaven

date
2004

media/techniques
collage, photography, adobe
photoshop

illustration (opposite)
he loves me, he loves me not

date
2003

media/techniques
collage, photography, adobe
photoshop

Béatrice Sautereau

birthplace Bordeaux, France
education School of Graphic Arts, Paris, France
inspiration Fernando Botero, Joan Miró, Pablo Picasso, classical painting

I was born in Bordeaux, France, and I studied at the École Supérieure d'Arts Graphiques (School of Graphic Arts) in Paris. I chose graphic arts because I have a passion for drawing and that is how I came to work in illustration.

I now work freelance. My clients have included *Marie Claire*, Italy, *Cosmo Girl*, USA and *Challenge*, a French economics magazine. I have also illustrated a children's book for the French publisher Éditions Nathan. I recently had an exhibition entitled 'Frivolous' at the Artazart Gallery in Paris.

I really like Fernando Botero, Joan Miró and Pablo Picasso, because of their sense of humour and simplicity. For me, Botero's work has grotesque sweetness. I like Miró for the way he combined delicate lines with large areas of colour. With Picasso, I love the variety in his work and how he continually managed to astonish at every period of his art.

I love fashion and beautiful things, but I often take my inspiration from everyday life. I try to be humourous in my work and try to play with the idea of beauty. I try to reproduce ordinary society in my images, and make people laugh at little details; for example, it could be a tooth in a smile, exaggerated make-up, a position or even the proportions. My representations of misshapen beauty and reality often surprise people. I like real people: I find a lot of variety in people's faces and body positions and I like reproducing these to give a richness to my work.

My inspiration is in the underground, in the streets, in photography and in magazines. I don't prepare preliminary sketches, instead I draw directly onto a computer using a digital pad. I draw using Adobe Photoshop software, always with a very fine line and using vibrant colours, as I find that bright, flat colours simplify what is essential about a character.

illustration
february 19th at artazart

date
2004

media/techniques
adobe photoshop

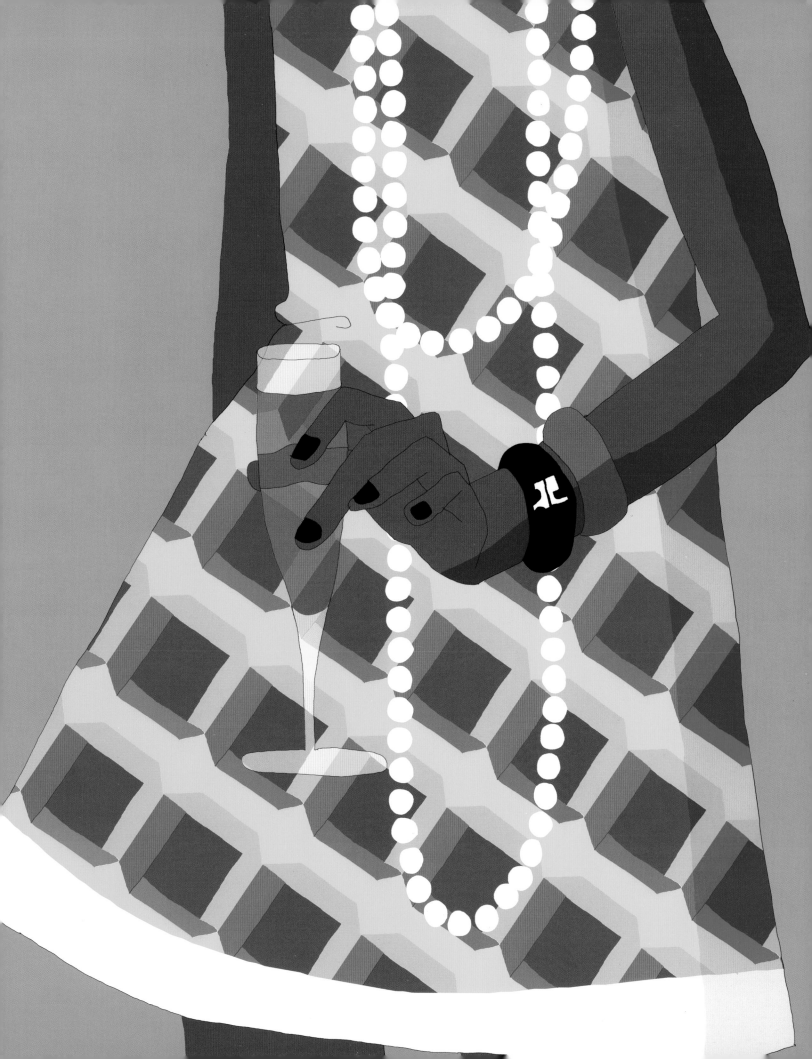

illustration
sales at selfridges

date
2004

media/techniques
adobe photoshop

illustration
fashion victims

date
2004

media/techniques
adobe photoshop

illustration
maria

date
2004

media/techniques
adobe photoshop

illustration
trevor

date
2004

media/techniques
adobe photoshop

illustration (opposite)
miss furbelows

date
2004

media/techniques
adobe photoshop

Sophie Robert

birthplace Vienne, France
education Ecole Duperrè, Paris, France
inspiration Paris, Marlene Dumas, Sofia Coppola, Marie Laurencin, Rineke Dijkstra

I was born in Vienne, near Lyon, France. First, I studied fashion design in Nîmes. Then I went to Paris to study fashion and environment at the Grande École of Applied Arts of Duperrè. I was still a student when the illustration agency Illustrissimo, in Paris, discovered my paintings and chose me to feature as the 'young talent' freelance artist on their website.

Paris is my inspiration, a divine city with a special atmosphere of charm and seduction (it is not a cliché!). Sitting on the terrace of a bar, drinking coffee, I like to observe the way people are dressed in the street, the way they are trying to seduce others with those 'little things' they are wearing. I try to remember them to use in my work, recreating a movement, an attitude … the little poetry that I witnessed. My illustrations are a kind of intimate Polaroid for me – a sort of 'happy nostalgia'.

I use a double-inking watercolour technique in order to produce these images. I first use a very pale, light watercolour to indicate the body posture and pose. I then use a black Chinese ink to fill in any details. The black ink intensifies the colours and really makes the characters and the clothes stand out. This technique corresponds to my own vision of fashion as something elusive. My fashion illustrations are light, volatile, ephemeral. They seek to capture a particular time, a period or an emotion – maybe a perfume, an essence – something feminine and concentrated on a paper.

illustration
at the café

date
2004

media/techniques
watercolour and black chinese
ink on paper

For me, watercolour is as light, sensual and superficial as fashion. I love the fragility of creating a figure or a little story using only water and a little bit of colour. Using water is essential for me: water is the first element on the paper; it is the possible illustration or the possible disaster. Even if I have an overall vision of the painting that I want to create, water is the real guide of my illustration; I have to adapt with its changing nature. But I love the idea that I am not the total master of illustration. This traditional painting technique will always fascinate and surprise me.

Sophie Robert

illustration (far left)
fashion week in paris

date
2004

media/techniques
watercolour, black chinese
ink and trichloréthylène printing
on paper

illustration (left)
the mirror

date
2004

media/techniques
watercolour and black chinese
ink on paper

illustration
the hotel

date
2004

media/techniques
watercolour and black chinese
ink on paper

Frédéric Desmots

birthplace Mantes la Jolie, Normandy, France
inspiration Nan Goldin, Richard Kern, Patrick Nagel

I live near the coast of Normandy in France. I have an unusual artistic background, as I did not study at an art school. I first painted for myself, without exhibiting my work. I created my own fantasy characters and comic strips, and also drew portraits of actors and singers. I worked on various surfaces, such as canvas or craft paper, using acrylics or pastels. I then went on to show my works in various local exhibitions. To take my work further and achieve the look I was after, I did a training course in desktop publishing. I spent a year experimenting with the software on my own to create a portfolio that I sent to various agencies.

Since then, I have illustrated articles for *BIBA* magazine, created portraits of celebrities for *Gloss* magazine, and worked on advertising campaigns for l'Oréal, Garnier, Suez, Bénédicta. I always knew I would work in graphic design. Even as a child, my main pastime was drawing. I always felt the need to create my own unique visual image.

I buy a lot of comic books, and particularly admire the work of Dave McKean, Jean-Michel Nicollet and Romain Slocombe. I like the dark side of Nicollet and McKean, the monstrosity of humanity, its hidden face and the mutation of men, and Slocombe for his work from photographs. The artist Patrick Nagel inspired me with his compositions, his stylish minimalism and the women that he painted. I have always oscillated between the black side of the comic book artists and glamour of Nagel. I also like the photographs of Nan Goldin and Richard Kern.

I work on a computer, using Adobe Photoshop or Adobe Illustrator with filters for a smooth yet realistic look, and add interesting textures. Most of the time my work is based on my own pictures of friends. I always begin my drawing on the top left-hand side, and then continue in an anticlockwise direction. I always finalize the character before anything else. From there the drawing can evolve harmoniously.

illustration
culture coach

date
2004

media/techniques
adobe photoshop, adobe
illustrator

I have tended toward minimalism more and more. To begin with, I was faithfully recreating every detail, but then I realized that just focusing on certain parts like the eyes, the nose and the mouth, was enough to make the face come alive. The image remains evocative. As the movie director Jacques Tati used to say: 'Too many colours distract the spectator.' I stay true to this formula myself by eliminating superfluous colours and details.

illustration
untitled

date
2004

media/techniques
adobe photoshop, adobe
illustrator

illustration
untitled

date
2004

media/techniques
adobe photoshop, adobe
illustrator

illustration
untitled

date
2004

media/techniques
adobe photoshop, adobe
illustrator

illustration
untitled

date
2004

media/techniques
adobe photoshop, adobe
illustrator

illustration
untitled

date
2004

media/techniques
adobe photoshop, adobe
illustrator

Stéphane Goddard

birthplace Chambéry, France
education School of Graphic Art, Lyon, France; ENSAAMA, Paris, France
inspiration Francis Bacon, Hugo Pratt, Diego da Silva y Velázquez, John Fante

I was born in the Alps, in Chambéry, France. I graduated from the School of Graphic Art, La Martinière, Lyon, and the ENSAAMA, Paris. I'm passionate about images, sports and nature. Actually, ever since I've been able to hold a pencil, I've drawn. It's like a compulsion. I adore drawing to create images that don't exist, inspired by reality, but not actually real.

I work regularly for newspapers and magazines and, in particular, with *Libération*, *Le Monde*, *ELLE*, *Les Inrock* and *L'Evénement du jeudi* alongside my position as creative director at a well-known Parisian advertising agency. I'm responsible for, among others, campaigns for Audi, Nike and Adidas. I've exhibited my work in Lyon's town hall, Le Citadium, a sports concept store, and in the Stade de France museum (French national stadium). I like to exhibit in unusual places, to reach out to ordinary people. I'm very proud to hear that my style is appreciated by a wide audience (from teenagers to old people) and by the next generation of illustrators.

My inspirations include: American comics, the artists Francis Bacon, Hugo Pratt and Diego da Silva y Velázquez, the writer John Fante, and film-makers David Lynch and the Cohen brothers. I like all these artists because they've created strong, beautiful, funny and inventive worlds. In fact, I find inspiration in everything: the street, music, cinema, photographs in magazines, books, people, nature. I like drawing people's fashion, not high fashion. I am inspired by the street. When drawing fashion, you can change and also imagine your own fashion styles. There isn't a conscious message in my work, but people can find their own meaning in it if they want to. I try to create the most beautiful, effective and emotional images I can.

illustration
mayday

date
2003

media/techniques
gouache, adobe photoshop

First, I start by researching ideas, and for this I produce lot of sketches. I select the strongest one. My sketches are very important; they guide me. I put colours directly on the white page. I like this method, it allows me to use colour to build 'the nervous system' of my image, without being a slave to drawing. I always battle with colours and materials to capture just the right shape and fix the strongest emotion. I usually paint only with gouache, but recently I've changed my style to encompass other techniques. I now use Adobe Photoshop to give the piece its finishing touches. I use my artworks and paintings, materials, fonts and personal photography sources, and scan them in at a very high resolution to make a digital collage. They are then reworked and enriched in texture and colour. This gives a whole new dynamic to the creative process.

illustration
bruce lyrics

date
2003

media/techniques
gouache, adobe photoshop

illustration
logan

date
2003

media/techniques
gouache, adobe photoshop

illustration
hotboard

date
2003

media/techniques
gouache, adobe photoshop

illustration
john doe

date
2003

media/techniques
gouache, adobe photoshop

Katrin Assman

birthplace Essen, Germany
education Folkwangschule für Gestaltung, Essen, Germany
inspiration Rolf Erlbruch, Stefanie Harjes, Brad Holland, David Hockney

I was born in Essen, Germany. I studied communication design at the Folkwangschule für Gestaltung in Essen. Today, I live with my daughter Karla and work as a freelance artist in Berlin and Los Angeles.

My illustrations have appeared in numerous magazines in the fields of fashion, politics and economics, in advertisements and also in children's books. I have also had exhibitions in Berlin and Spain.

I developed my style while studying design at the Folkwangschule, a university that teaches in the tradition of the Bauhaus movement. On the course, we learn to have our own judgement about art and design and also to have a subjective point of view and taste. We were not taught to work in a given style, but rather to develop our independence in our work. The focus was on the process of the work.

For me, this process is a playful and spontaneous one, which often surprises me. I don't have a definite image in my mind when I start the illustration and very often I ignore the objective of the work. The client's request is the initial trigger for finding the idea. I consider the work of an illustrator to be a service rather than artistic self-realization. Very often, it is the most unexpected ideas that convey the message in the best way.

I use Chinese ink for the black lines but use a variety of materials, such as pencil, watercolour, acrylic and marker pens, for colour. I also have a vast library of clippings and bits and pieces from all kinds of magazines and other sources that I use for my collages. Different clippings from photographs out of magazines provide additional textures and colours for the dresses and parts of the background. The jewellery in my illustrations are from catalogues and I have even used giftwrap and string for greater variety of colour and texture. Sometimes I take clippings from older paintings and illustrations that I don't need anymore and are overpainted and altered in some areas. In places the paint is scratched away to add more texture. I'm not too precious about my originals and so once an image is printed it might get recycled to become part of something new.

illustration
luxury 1

date
1998

media/techniques
collage, marker pen, chinese ink

It is important to me that the illustration is direct, so that the viewer is able to understand the statement of the work immediately. It should steer the senses rather than being abstract and difficult to access. Here, I distinguish between my fashion and lifestyle artworks and my illustrations for political publications. In the latter, you need to convince with an idea. With fashion illustrations other things are more important. The choice of colour, technique and line tend to be much more determined by trends.

illustration
invitation 1

date
1999

media/techniques
collage, pencil, watercolour,
acrylic

illustration
invitation 2

date
1999

media/techniques
collage, pencil, watercolour,
acrylic

illustration
luxury 2

date
1998

media/techniques
collage, marker pen, chinese ink

Kai Bardeleben

birthplace Hamburg, Germany
education Waldoerfer Gymnasium Volksdorf, Germany
inspiration Ludwig Hohlwein, Fernand Léger, Jean Dupas, Tamara De Lempicka

The 1920s and 1930s Art Deco movement has always held a special place in my heart. Fashion, form, style and architecture were always expressed to perfection during this period, and who embodies this better, in all its glory, than the paintings of Tamara De Lempicka? How could I resist doing a fashion illustration series in that manner? The basic equipment for painting in that style is a canvas in the original measurements of her better-known works – often 140 x 70cm (55 x 28in). I abandoned the sweet, doll-type faces of that decade and supplied instead a modern face of my own creation in order to update that era to our own millennium.

I tend to use the same models over and over again, and have painted some of them for years – so often, in fact, that I can often paint completely from memory. Painting to me, therefore, always feels more like sculpting a statue than painting on canvas.

If I am not painting from memory or from still life I work from photography. The digital camera is a wonderful instrument to have when facing the time shortages we encounter today. Also absolutely essential is a 500-watt light bulb, which enables you to work in daylight conditions whatever the time of day or night.

I can usually visualize from the beginning how I want my paintings to look when they are complete. I reduce the figure to parts of light and shade with only flecks of highlights on it to define the plasticity, as seen in paintings by Ludwig Hohlwein, for example. For time reasons I begin the first layers of a painting using acrylic paint, and only use oils during the later stages as they take a long time to dry.

illustration
heidi

date
1996

media/techniques
oil on canvas

I am always careful to keep my subjects monochrome, to underline the statuesque nature of the character and to reduce their charm and beauty to its most simple, distilled form. For final adjustments I keep the model in the studio for a few hours, where she models for me in the flesh and in colour.

illustration
portrait 'julia'

date
1998

media/techniques
oil on canvas

illustration (left)
self portrait

date
2003

media/techniques
acrylic on canvas

Albert Morell

birthplace Bremen, Germany
education Academy of Arts, Kassel, Germany
inspiration Helmut Newton, Jason Brooks, Adolphe Cassandre, David Hockney

I was born in Bremen, Germany, and grew up in an artistic home. My father, Pit Morrell, is a painter, and drawing and creativity was encouraged from an early age. I studied at and then graduated from the Academy of Arts, Kassel, Germany and continued to develop new ideas and techniques while working for a year in Paris. I now live and work in Berlin.

The style of my portraits is based upon my fascination with the human face, combined with the use of clear outlines and simple colouration. When I see an interesting face, a certain attitude, a certain look, it's not so much about youth, but about the sensuality and sensibility seen in the face. Normally I take photographs, or cut faces out of a magazine or a book. The next step is to lay a transparent paper over the chosen image and sketch all the main outlines of the face with a fine brush and black ink, including all details such as eyes, nose and mouth. Then I make a scan of this drawing and convert the scan into a black and white graphic image using Adobe Streamline. Now I complete the illustration in a vector-based graphic program, adding all the colours and finishing with shadows and lights. I create several versions of the same motif, each in different colour combinations.

Changing the colour of the eyes or the hair gives me greater flexibility to pick and choose the best version – something that would have been impossible before digital graphic programs came on the market. What I like most about this technique is the hand-made look that the finished illustrations have, without looking too realistic or artificial. All my techniques are mixed media and computer aided, so my pictures are really nothing more than a kind of snapshot photograph.

When exhibiting my work I usually display between 10 and 18 portraits. They are large, ink-jet colour prints about 128cm (50in) wide and printed on canvas material. The canvas gives them the look of an original, but as they are reproductions they are not too expensive to make and can be sold at reasonable prices.

My work is largely influenced by the visual language of advertising posters from the 1920s to the 1950s, which have fascinated me since childhood. I like their simple, colourful surfaces and their astonishing graphic composition. I find that Erté, the Russian-born French designer and artist, epitomizes the elegance and style of the fashion illustrations of this era. He was one of the most highly regarded and influential of artists of the early 20th century, and his work has appeared everywhere, from theatrical opera stage sets to interior design, from advertising campaigns to fashion and costume design for film productions. What I like about Erté is his unique style, the harmony of colours and the elegance and perfection of the lines. On the one hand, his work is accurate and disciplined and on the other, it displays artistic extravagance and rich fantasy. He represents the glamour of a long-forgotten time, and stands for a successful marriage between art and commerce. He's also kitsch.

illustration
hermes orange dufflecoat

date
2002

media/techniques
vectorgraphic

Today, it is hard to create your own unique style. With so many changing trends, short-term fashions and various imitations, it's important for me to stay true to my own style. Following too many trends slavishly can be a dead end for creativity. But I should also say that being an illustrator is all about fun!

illustration (opposite)
portrait of german photographer
joachim baldauf

date
2002

media/techniques
vectorgraphic

illustration (above)
portrait with wallpaper

date
2002

media/techniques
vectorgraphic

Giulio Iurissevich

birthplace Pordenone, Italy
education Università degli Studi di Trieste, Trieste, Italy
inspiration Danjel Zezelj, Salvador Dali, Pablo Picasso, Egon Schiele, Alphonse Mucha

I was born in Pordenone, a little town close to Venice, in Italy, in 1972. After studying law at university I decided to return to my first passion: drawing and making pictures. I began as a graphic designer making flyers, calendars and catalogues. Now I'm a self-taught artist and freelance illustrator, specializing in fashion, people and lifestyle illustration. I have worked with a wide variety of clients from around the world, especially in the UK, USA and Germany.

As child I grew up with my favourite comics, Topolino and Alan Ford, and spent a lot of time taking photographs with my father, who is very keen on photography. When I was about 16 I discovered one of the best comics ever produced, *Sun City* by Danjel Zezelj, which began a life-long passion for illustration and design.

Zezelj is still my favourite artist, although I also love Salvador Dali and Pablo Picasso, as well as Egon Schiele and Alphonse Mucha. However, I draw most of my inspiration from the world around me. I'm inspired by the music I listen to, by magazines and films I've seen, and by people I see every day. I have always loved people, and this is the reason for my approach to fashion illustration.

Although my first love remains photography, I find a freedom in illustration that is not possible in other mediums. Through photography and my USB tablets I discovered Adobe Photoshop and work mostly in digital now, on my computer. I often use photographs as a starting point for design work, and like to play with the geometry of the image. I also use Adobe Photoshop to adjust volumes and colours. I make use of quite similar colours, which is a constant in my work, and often like to draw in black and white. However, I prefer clean lines to using effects, and for this reason I work mainly in Adobe Illustrator, particularly when representing people. Illustration is different from photography because you create something that has never existed before, adding and changing various elements according to your imagination. I make a free-hand rough draft of my final work, then I digitalize and vectorialize that using Adobe Illustrator with my USB tablet.

It usually takes around four or five days to complete a piece of work, although I'm driven by instinct and stop only when I recognize myself in my pictures. For me the most important part is to leave a sign, or a personal stamp, on the work. I always strive to create an interpretation of the world that communicates my views and style. I think this is the reason I'm an illustrator, to express myself.

Anyone who chooses to do this kind of work must have great passion and nerves of steel. It's not easy, but the trick is to love your work. Believe in what you do, practise constantly and see the work of the others. For me my work is a necessity, a need to communicate what I am, and the best way for me to express myself is through my work.

illustration
stop!

date
2003

media/techniques
adobe photoshop, adobe illustrator

illustration
breakdance

date
2004

media/techniques
adobe photoshop, adobe illustrator

Tatjana Jeremic

birthplace Stockholm, Sweden
education Beckman's School of Design, Stockholm, Sweden
inspiration Helmut Newton, Betty Brader, Lilla Rogers, Anna Sui

I live and work in Stockholm, Sweden – one of the world's most beautiful and inspiring cities if you ask me! As a little girl, I was constantly sketching and drawing, determined to one day fulfil the dream of working as a fashion designer or artist. In 1997, I graduated from Beckman's School of Design in Stockholm and was awarded the Milli McNaughton Award for best fashion illustration; an honour that undeniably spurred me on to pursue a career as a freelance illustrator.

My work has been exhibited at various Swedish galleries and is also represented in the book *The Best Swedish Fashion Illustrations of the Century*. My clientele typically consists of fashion magazines and advertising firms, primarily Swedish, for whom I design textile patterns, clothing and advertisements. For example, I recently finished a project for the Swedish clothing chain Lindex for their loyalty club campaign.

I find inspiration all around me – for example, at museums, in photographs and from magazines. I do not have a particular artist or designer that I favour, but rather I find myself inspired by various individual pieces of artwork.

In my work as an illustrator, I strive to continually surprise myself with the results. I am a very emotional person and my drawings are finished when they 'feel' done. That is to say, when they 'speak' to me, expressing life and emotion. There is always a particular feeling I strive for with an illustration and, to achieve it, I find myself using a variety of techniques on a single piece of work.

illustration
passion

date
2003

media/techniques
adobe photoshop

Each project begins with a long period of research, before I proceed to the sometimes tedious phase of creating quick sketches until I get the right 'feel'. Behind each of my illustrations there is, on average, a pile of 70–80 discarded sketches. After the initial sketch has been fleshed out, I scan it and begin working on it using Adobe Photoshop. I select a soft, but fresh range of colours that would draw interest to the clothing itself. In addition, I scan flowers and petals from different plants, adding these to the illustrations for texture and interest. I do a lot of cutting and pasting until everything falls into place and I feel satisfied with the result. I find that my illustrations always turn out the best when the client gives me freedom during the creative process.

illustration
classic

date
2003

media/techniques
adobe photoshop

illustration
glamour

date
2003

media/techniques
adobe photoshop

illustration
lingerie

date
2003

media/techniques
adobe photoshop

Karen Oxman

birthplace Haifa, Israel
education Bezalel Academy of Arts, Jerusalem; Royal College of Art, London
inspiration August Sander, Alice Neel, Giotto di Bondone, Rei Kawakubo

By the time I was 18, I had lived in four different countries. I was born in Israel; after that there was the Netherlands, Australia and the United States. This constant change of environments makes a young person extremely sensitive to her own place in any given cultural space. It is a kaleidoscopic experience that enriches your visual world tremendously.

I studied communication art and design at St Martins, London, and at the Bezalel Academy of Arts in Jerusalem, where I graduated with honours. Following Bezalel, and as result of work done there and since, I was awarded the prestigious Clore Scholarship to pursue advanced studies at the Royal College of Arts in London. At the moment I am living in New York City and freelancing on a range of illustration projects for books, magazines and CDs.

In my teens, I was surrounded by fashion magazines and thus was exposed to fashion as a form of modern expression even before I was aware of fashion as a cultural phenomenon. I used these magazines as an inspiration for drawing, so the connection between art and fashion came about very naturally. By redrawing fashion images, I personalized them and made them my own. Gradually, I became interested in drawing as the main event, leaving the images behind. The residue of those sources still resonates in my work.

Today's fashion is a world dominated by photographers and photography. It is a visual world. I try to capture this visual reality in my work. I am interested in the artistic potential of life seen as style, the poetics of the fashion image as a prototype for experience. I enjoy the playfulness and irony of juxtaposing reality, fantasy and abstraction. I attempt to create the poetical, lyrical world within a contemporary condition. The images evoke the anonymity, aloofness and distance of 18th-century portrait paintings, through the ironic glare of a modern eye.

I have noticed that some interesting things happen after I have already laid out my initial idea. Once a sketch is done, there is still room for surprises and good accidents to occur. In other words, I don't 'marry' the sketch. I use it as a guide, or a map, but not as a linear version of the final image.

illustration
blush

date
2003

media/techniques
adobe photoshop

I try to explore the borderline between painting, collage and computer media. I often start with a loose sketch in the computer, using flat-coloured silhouettes, trying to arrange the core elements of the image. These can include the placement of the head, a general feel for the pose, a clue to what the background might be, and some basic colour combination that defines the general atmosphere. In this early stage there is a role for intuition which lends the work a certain spontaneity. When the composition is set, I start working on refining the image and its visual content. I look for abstract shapes that enrich the setting of the image. I scan in two-dimensional elements and make them flat shapes in Adobe Photoshop. To add another dimension to the image I also scan in paintings or photographs and use them as fragments of collage inside the image. I also paint directly in Adobe Photoshop, mostly using the brush and smudge tools, making the focus shift to certain areas. I try to blend all of these techniques in the digital image as seamlessly as possible.

illustration
girl in black

date
2003

media/techniques
adobe photoshop

illustration
dusk

date
2003

media/techniques
adobe photoshop

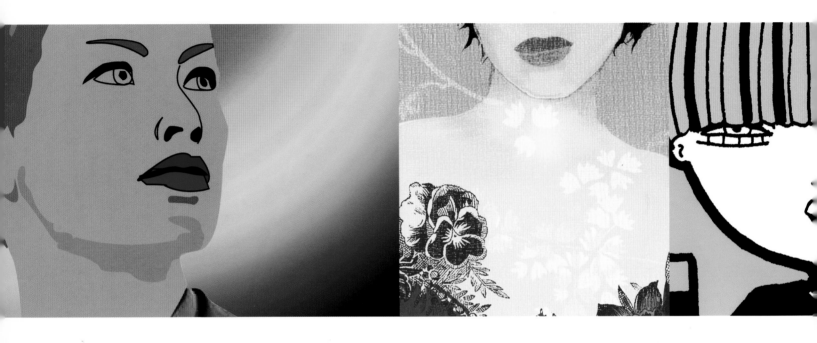

North & South
America

Kalani Lee

birthplace Savannah, Georgia, USA
education Rutgers University, Newark, New Jersey, USA
inspiration Andy Warhol, RuPaul, Shirley Manson, Twiggy

When I was a kid, my family moved to exotic places across Asia, Europe and the United States with the Army, so I learnt to appreciate the cultural diversity of the world. I currently live in New York City, constantly drawing inspiration from my surroundings. Whether it is from the street kids on St Mark's Place, the beautiful transsexuals on Christopher Street or the chic hipster shops in Soho, I'm amazed by the variety and energy of this gorgeous city.

The people who interest me the most (aesthetically) embody a sense of style that is backed up by their personalities and not the other way around. Andy Warhol, Bjork, RuPaul, Shirley Manson, David Bowie and Patti Smith are great examples. They're all very intense and eccentric individuals in their own right.

My fashion characters have been described as 'fantasy girls with pouty lips and bedroom eyes'. I like to think of them as illustrated models whose purpose is to convey an attitude. Whether it is cute, sexy, edgy, androgynous, playful or all of the above, the clothing, accessories and hairstyle combine to project a particular mood and fashion style.

Before starting any project, I flesh out the persona of the characters. As my ideas progress, they turn into pencil sketches, bubble heads, stick-figure bodies and scribbled ideas and phrases describing what the image should look like. After getting the feel of the basic composition, I draw another draft, adding details like hairstyle, accessories and clothing to suit the particular fashion style. For example, if I'm drawing a Punk girl, I might give her a shaved head, a torn T-shirt with an anti-establishment logo, tight leather jeans and black combat boots or maybe go in a different direction. It all depends whether the client wants something specific or whether I'm given creative freedom. I then complete the semi-final outline with a pencil, fixing mistakes and adding last-minute details. The final outline can be traced with whatever medium best portrays my models (subtle, hard, feminine, masculine), and I enjoy experimenting with crayon, marker, watercolour, gouache, script pen and Indian ink. The final illustration is then scanned, manipulated and coloured on my computer in Adobe Photoshop.

illustration
march

date
2004

media/techniques
pen, adobe photoshop

I think that a great fashion illustration is one that is so eye-catching that the viewer feels compelled to rip it out of the magazine or to buy the product it is endorsing. Maybe they can relate to the style or maybe they just think it's cute. Who knows? Personally, I'm guilty of buying a magazine for a fashion illustration alone.

illustration (left)
she's got it

date
2004

media/techniques
sharpie, marker pen, adobe
photoshop

illustration (right)
dandelion girl

date
2003

media/techniques
indian ink, gouache, adobe
photoshop

Jonathan deLagarde

birthplace Queens, New York City, USA
education New York University, New York City, USA
inspiration Amos Ferguson, Jean-Michel Basquiat, Frank Miller, Futura 2000

I was born in Queens, New York City. Growing up, I had so many influences – so many things helped to round out my view of the world and how to interpret it creatively. I have lived in both urban and suburban areas. I read voraciously. Growing up in my house, the two major expressions were music and art. Jazz, calypso, classical, reggae, hip-hop – you name it, it was played. I remember at an early age being inspired by Amos Ferguson, a Bohemian artist who my father was fond of. I discovered the artist and graffitist Jean-Michel Basquiat, and was drawn to the graphic novels of Frank Miller, especially his epic work *The Dark Knight Returns*. I discovered the genius of the graffiti artists Futura 2000 and Dondi White (whose precision pencil work I particularly admire). Then I became enamoured with animated works such as *Akira*, *Heavy Metal* and, later, *Ghost in the Shell*. The futuristic clothing that the animators have drawn in these movies is an inspiration for my own work.

At the moment, I am designing clothes for Gap and for my own line Delagarde. In the past, I have designed for a diverse client list that includes Sony Music, MeccaUSA, Fila, BlueNotes and Starter.

My method varies when it comes to creating art. Sometimes I'm really focused and I force myself to sit down and sketch until the lead runs out! Other times I might be walking down the street, or watching a football game, and suddenly have to scramble for the sketchpad because an idea has manifested. Because I'm always sketching or scribbling something, I take a quick-handed style and approach to my finished work. The art I produce has a rough, jagged look that I love. It has a rawness to it that helps the viewer to appreciate it both as a means for communicating clothing design and as a conceptual art piece.

I love the simplicity of mediums such as pencil, charcoal and watercolour. All my illustrations start as pencil sketches on vellum or tracing paper. But I also enjoy the freedom I get when I scan in a pencil sketch and then manipulate like a mad scientist in Adobe Illustrator, which gives the piece that extra edge that makes it look complete. I scan the sketch into Adobe Photoshop, then use Adobe Streamline, then bring it in to Adobe Illustrator for colouring and fine tuning. But the initial pencil sketch is pretty similar to the finished product. I love using the masking technique in Adobe Illustrator. I use it to seamlessly place a true denim texture inside the outline of the clothing. Before I scan the denim swatch, I apply bleach to the denim, wait a few seconds, then iron it to give a blotched, weathered look. I also use other textures such as Microfleece, and find that skin tones can be recreated by scanning in Cabretta leather, the leather most often used to make golf gloves.

The one thing that helps my work stand out is to draw inspiration from inside my head. Although I devour books and magazines, I try to eliminate all those influences, trust my instincts, and follow my mind and soul.

illustration
leisurely

date
2003

media/techniques
pencil, charcoal, adobe illustrator, adobe streamline

illustration
problem child

date
2003

media/techniques
pencil, charcoal, adobe
illustrator, adobe streamline

illustration
horace

date
2004

media/techniques
pencil, charcoal, adobe
illustrator, adobe streamline

illustration (far left)
redemption

date
2003

media/techniques
pencil, charcoal, adobe
illustrator, adobe streamline

illustration (left)
nesta

date
2004

media/techniques
pencil, charcoal, adobe
illustrator, adobe streamline

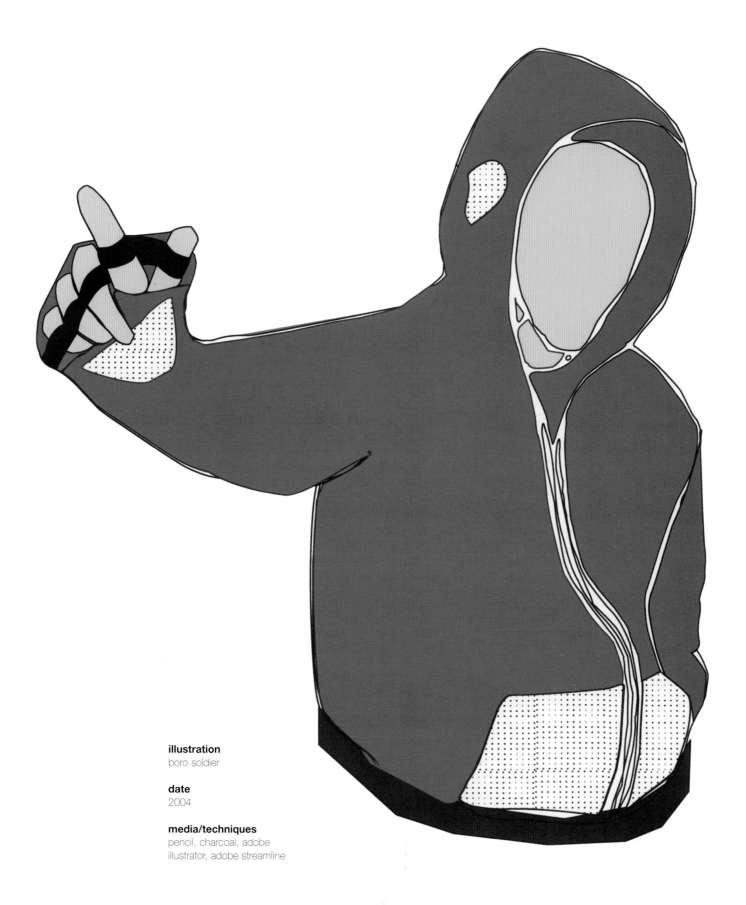

illustration
boro soldier

date
2004

media/techniques
pencil, charcoal, adobe
illustrator, adobe streamline

Lisa Henderling

birthplace New York City, USA
education High School of Art and Design, New York City, USA; Fashion Institute of Technology, New York City, USA
inspiration Antonio Lopez, modern architecture, furniture design, New York City

I was born in New York City and wanted to be a commercial artist since I was five. All I wanted to do was take art lessons and to draw. I would wait for advertisements by my favourite illustrators to appear in magazines and then I would try to copy them.

I always thought the fashion illustrator, Antonio Lopez, was a genius. I watched him draw once and the drawing flowed out of him as effortlessly as breathing. It was beautiful to watch. He always changed his style and moved on to something new – he never got stuck in a formula.

I went to the High School of Art and Design, New York City, and Fashion Institute of Technology, New York City. Although I was trained in fashion illustration, I have done many other types of drawing. I love to draw, but to be a commercial artist it is essential that you are responsible to your clients and deadlines – having discipline and a sense of business is as important as being talented. I now freelance full time for clients such as Hasbro, Nordstrom, Snapple, Anheuser Bush, Jergens, Borders, Kimberly Clark, *New York Times*, *Wall Street Journal*, Girl Scouts of America, American Express, Avon, Taco Bell and many more.

I would say that my illustrations are graphic, stylized, sophisticated and light-hearted. I like to present an idea of fashion, or a fashion lifestyle, rather than show every detail of clothing that a photograph would capture. I like hanging out with people who are involved in some form of the arts, it always inspires me, and I am always looking at what is happening in music, fashion and interior design, as well as on the street, on TV and in magazines. It is important to stay interested and up to date with current trends and to always keep growing and trying new ideas out. This is always reflected in the work and keeps the designs looking fresh.

illustration
annabelle

date
2003

media/techniques
adobe illustrator

I also look at photographs for inspiration, and for a pose, but I don't directly imitate anything. I do many rough hand drawings and start all over again lots of times! The most important part of the illustration is the design, or the way things are laid out on the page. I do lots of loose sketches before I come up with a composition I like. Once I get that right then I move on to refining the figures. I would say my style is very designed. I like to work loosely initially and then refine the illustration until I am left with simple shapes. Once I am happy with the pencil rough I scan it into the computer. Then I work on setting up my colour palette. I never do colour studies; I prefer to experiment as I go along. I work in three layers in the layer palette, naming them tracing, colour and background. Then I just delete my hand-drawn rough tracing layer when I am finished. I also use Adobe Illustrator's pre-set patterns and change their colours or alter them in some way. I use the mouse for drawing. Learning how to draw is still the most important thing in illustration and fashion illustration. No amount of computer knowledge will compensate for lack of drawing skills.

I love to draw! I think this is the most important part of the design process. If there is a message in my work it is simply to have fun!

94

illustration
fashionista

date
2004

media/techniques
adobe illustrator

illustration
yoga

date
2004

media/techniques
adobe illustrator

illustration (opposite)
sporty

date
2004

media/techniques
adobe illustrator

illustration
downtown chic

date
2004

media/techniques
adobe illustrator

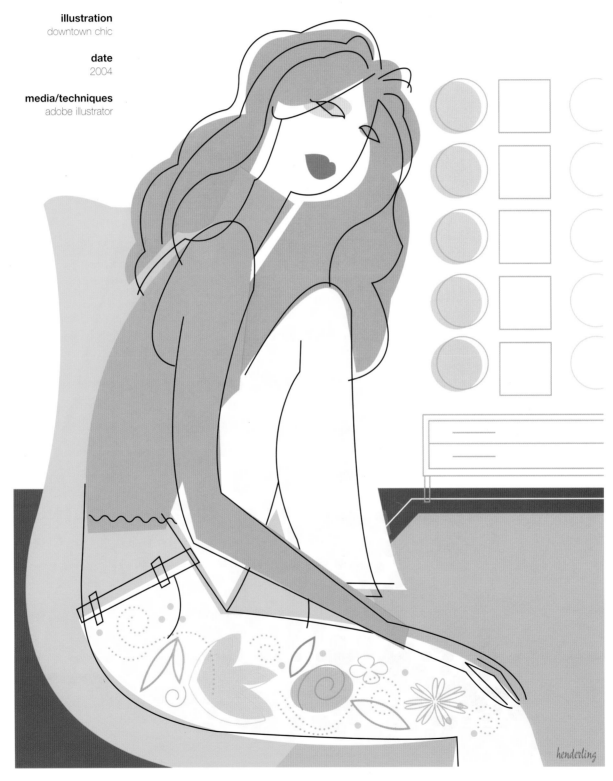

illustration
wild-at-heart

date
2004

media/techniques
adobe illustrator

Autumn Whitehurst

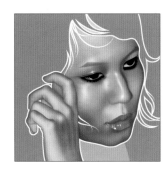

birthplace Providence, Rhode Island, USA
education Maryland Institute College of Art, USA
inspiration Katsushika Hokusai, Hans Bellmer, George Grosz

I grew up in New Orleans, in the United States. When I think about my childhood, I think about how much heat influenced my cultural upbringing – we ate hot-weather foods, listened to sleepy, hot-weather music, lived in a house built to accommodate the heat, and I rarely left my bedroom to avoid sweating to death, which amounted to lots of reading and drawing. As a result I spent the majority of my time living inside my head. I ended up attending the Maryland Institute College of Art where I found a voice through oil painting. It's still my first love, though I haven't had the time to paint as, for the past couple of years, I have been busy with my efforts to establish myself as an illustrator.

When I began putting my portfolio together, I vaguely knew that I wanted to focus on fashion but tried various things to widen my range. I hadn't intended to focus on figures initially but a commission from US fashion brand Ecko Red, for an illustration of a young woman glazed in sweat for an advertisement campaign, set me off in that direction. That illustration has come to define the way that I'm presently working, which is pretty much a marriage between what the computer allows me to do and what I can impose upon the computer. It gives me the ability to play until I'm really finished.

My work is entirely digital, from the initial sketches to the final rendering. I take photographs as references for the way light falls on a three-dimensional figure, and then I lay out the line work in Adobe Illustrator, later bringing it into Adobe Photoshop to create the skin tones using the brushes. Generally, I'm more fanatical about playing with line and colour than I am about rendering the figure. Although it may not seem that way, the rendering is actually only there to place emphasis on the lines. My technique is very similar to drawing or painting with traditional media, except that my tools are my computer and my Wacom tablet. The majority of my effort is spent in imagining and creating an idealized body or face. Lines and colours are required to make up for the restrictions created by working so tightly with the human form. In the near future, I plan to take my work further by loosening up and allowing for more mishaps. I'd like to push it more to divorce it from photography and to really take advantage of its potential as an illustration.

illustration
glossy

date
2004

media/techniques
adobe photoshop, adobe illustrator

Much of what has influenced my aesthetics, especially my love for lines, is the result of having an Asian mother. I don't know if it's a genetic predisposition or a cultural influence but I really can't help myself. I have an enormous amount of respect for Hokusai but also for such artists as Hans Bellmer and George Grosz. Their work is simply beautiful. I was told once that you can't argue with beauty and really, I think that's true.

illustration (above)	illustration (opposite)	illustration (next page)
j is for jewellery	bride	dandelions
date	**date**	**date**
2003	2004	2004
media/techniques	**media/techniques**	**media/techniques**
adobe photoshop, adobe illustrator	adobe photoshop, adobe illustrator	adobe photoshop, adobe illustrator

Fawn Gehweiler

birthplace Miami, Florida, USA
inspiration Shelly Duvall, Igor Pantuhoff, Vera Chytilova, Mary Blair, textile design

From nearly being born in a boat off the coast of Jamaica to spending the first few years of my life on a perpetual road trip, and finally, growing up in the mountains of Hawaii sans electricity, a spirit of adventure and innate wanderlust were instilled in me at an early age. Consequently, the years since have found me in any number of US cities, from New York to San Francisco, and a million points in between.

My illustration clients have included Levi's, VH1, Warner Brothers, and a variety of national and international magazines and record labels. My work has also appeared in a number of design books and annuals, and in galleries across the US, Europe and Japan. My current favourite project is an ongoing campaign for the New York vintage clothing boutique Screaming Mimi's; a series of monthly print advertisements where I get to place my characters in fanciful locales wearing the vintage clothing trends of the season.

Described by *FACE* magazine as 'the visual equivalent of candyfloss peppered with broken glass – delicious yet dangerous', my characters are borne out of an infinite loop of life-imitates-art-imitates-life, ad infinitum. For example, some of my earliest characters were based on the ongoing story of a 1960s delinquent girl gang, based on myself and my friends. Eventually, this project took on a life of its own, with a series of comic books, membership cards, nationwide chapters, T-shirts, and even an exhibition. Ever since, my characters have always embodied at least some element of me – a current obsession, collection or emerging fashion statement – which makes even the most commercial assignments fun, and keeps them vital and interesting.

All of my fine art evolves in a similar way, with little notes and tiny sketches on scraps of paper, bits of napkins and gum wrappers, cryptic notes and top ten lists. The characters evolve organically out of these influences. All my pieces are painted on glass with enamels and acrylics, a technique I developed in order to avoid having brushstrokes or texture in my paintings – I later learned that this technique was actually a popular style in Europe at the turn of the century. I use a very limited, almost monochromatic palette, in order to maintain a consistent look throughout. Also, using the deeper colours as backgrounds lends a considerably darker feel to the work, which has a nice effect, and provides a perfect balance to the freckle-faced cuteness and implied sweetness of the characters.

My influences are flung far and wide, but some of my all-time favourites are otherworldly beauties like Pippi Longstocking and Twiggy, as well as eccentrics throughout history, from Marchesa Luisa Casati to Vivienne Westwood. I'm madly in love with the wispy Parisians of Igor Pantuhoff's paintings and everything that artist and designer Mary Blair has ever done. I have a huge collection of vintage children's books that are a constant source of inspiration and wonderment. My collections in general play a big part in shaping the world that is reflected in my artwork. For instance, I'm obsessed with 1960s and 1970s Avon product and packaging design, and being surrounded by it as I work probably informs my design decisions more than I can possibly imagine.

illustration
I want candy

date
2002

media/techniques
enamel and acrylic on glass

My work is always rooted in enthusiasm for current and newly discovered obsessions and inspirations. A cheap flea market find like a big-eyed doll or bit of fabric will send me straight to the sketchbooks in a flurry to map out a whole new world, awash with childhood nostalgia, full of new directions and possibilities. Everything from an advertisement campaign to a painting starts the same way, with an ever-evolving series of sketches, which eventually coagulate into exactly what they're meant to be.

illustration
bubblegum lolita

date
2002

media/techniques
enamel and acrylic on glass

illustration
electro girls and skycars

date
2002

media/techniques
enamel and acrylic on glass

Jen Renninger

birthplace Tampa, Florida, USA
education University of Miami, USA; Rochester Institute of Technology, USA
inspiration Rachel Salomon, Autumn Whitehurst, Andy Goldsworthy, Kiki Smith

I was raised in Tampa, Florida, and although I have lived in various other parts of the US, I have now settled back in the south. I have been a bibliophile since I was young; the pictures in magazines and books have always been a source of inspiration for me, but I only started illustrating about six years ago – almost on a whim. While studying for a postgraduate degree in fine art photography at the University of Miami, I realized I wasn't happy with the labels and restrictive ways in which the art world works. I didn't like being forced to show work that fits into a specific category; catering to a market was fine, but having to do it under the guise of being a self-guided artist wasn't. It really just seemed false, so I turned to the things that had given me inspiration for so many years: books and magazines. I decided that I would rather have my pictures in those pages than on gallery walls, so I set out to become an illustrator.

Looking back, it seems ridiculously easy, but I think it was really a matter of being ignorant enough to try anything. My undergraduate degree was actually in commercial photography and one class had been devoted to the process of working with art directors. This gave me enough of a foundation to get started: I went to the bookshop, plucked all the magazines I liked off the shelves, and wrote down the art directors' names and addresses. Within a week, I was a freelance illustrator. And I've been lucky enough that the work has been fairly consistent since then.

Artists and designers whose work I admire and other sources of inspiration? Now that's a list that could go on and on! Some of my favourite illustrators are Joel Holland, Rachel Salomon, Autumn Whitehurst and Jo Tyler. From the world of fine art, I love Andy Goldsworthy and Kiki Smith. I am continually inspired by independent publishers: those great people at McSweeney's really put out innovative publications and *Visionaire* is incredible as something that is both inspirational and more of a work of art than an ephemeral product.

As far as my own work goes, I feel as if it is still taking shape and finding its form stylistically. Ideally, I would like to create something that resonates with the viewer, something that lingers. I imagine that is probably what all image-makers want. Technically, I tend to work in the same manner for nearly all my illustrations: I do multiple sketches of the subject and then scan those sketches into Adobe Photoshop. Although I work digitally, I do start each picture with numerous sketches and rough paintings. More often than not, I end up taking parts of different sketches and piecing them together to make one final subject, the way you might put together a puppet, with an arm here, or a leg there. It's usually just a matter of reacting to line weight, or an elegant section of drawing that would complement another drawing.

illustration
lace

date
2003

media/techniques
watercolour, gouache, tape, ink, graphite, adobe photoshop

After my drawing has been brought together I bring in background colour. The patterning is always the final part of the illustration and I piece together a loose pattern that brings together all the other elements. For this I usually paint a texture or pattern on a piece of board and then scan it in. I sometimes layer many backgrounds together in Adobe Photoshop to get the combination that sets the right mood for the illustration. For me, this is where the image either succeeds or fails, and tends to be where I spend most of my time.

In all honesty, I feel so lucky to have stumbled into this profession. I love what I do and the people I work with. What could be better than that?

illustration
the bird cage

date
2002

media/techniques
watercolour, gouache, tape, ink,
graphite, adobe photoshop

illustration
high heel

date
2002

media/techniques
watercolour, gouache, tape, ink,
graphite, adobe photoshop

illustration
silk

date
2003

media/techniques
watercolour, gouache, tape, ink,
graphite, adobe photoshop

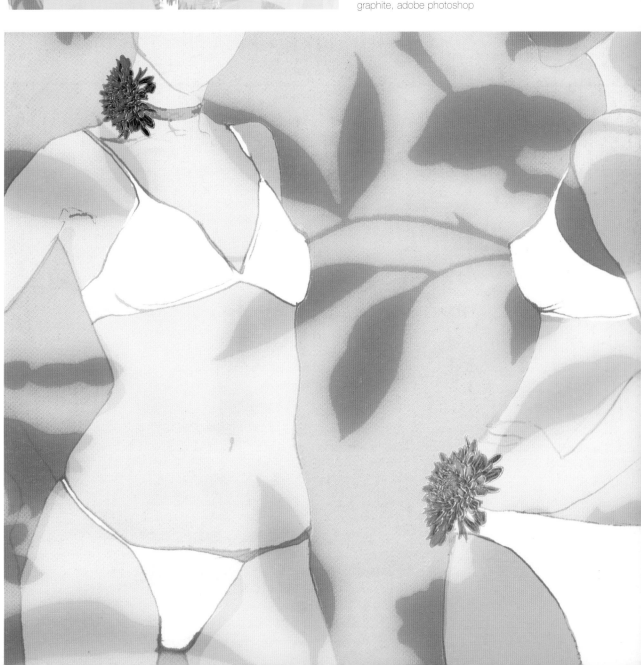

Jeff Spokes

birthplace Saskatoon, Saskatchewan, Canada
education School of Art and Design, New York City, USA; Fashion Institute of Technology, New York City, USA
inspiration Georgia O'Keeffe, Douglas Fraser, Gary Kelley, Steve McCurry

I was born Saskatoon, Saskatchewan, Canada. The process of image-making has interested me for as long as I can remember. Most of my fourth year of life was spent tracing at a window with a blank piece of paper taped over the top of a page torn from a *Star Wars* colouring book. I soon realized that if I could copy the lines in the colouring book page by just looking and then drawing, I could not only copy what I saw but make my own images by combining and drawing elements from a number of colouring book pages. Thus my career as an image-maker began.

What I enjoy most about image-making is the process of breathing in everything around me, and filtering it down into pictures. To list all my inspirations could take days, but the essentials would include the record company Real World Records, the painter Georgia O'Keeffe and musicians Michael Brook and Daniel Lanios. Other inspirations are the illustrators Alphonse Mucha, Douglas Fraser, Gary Kelley, and Mark Gervais; the photographers Steve McCurry and Anton Corbjin; comic book artist Mike Mignola and film-makers Ridley Scott, Michael Mann and P T Anderson.

I am fascinated with the film-making process and try to bring a bit of that influence into my work. With film, any given shot will comprise a staggering number of elements: an actor's performance, scale models, stage sets, background paintings, digital technology, film colour treatments, soundtrack. All these elements are then stitched together into one working image.

In the same way, when I start an image, it begins with an initial sketch that hammers out the character, pose and clothing. Then I gather references. I have a fairly large reference library, where I can find clothing, faces, colour palettes, lighting effects, objects, animals and so on, or I use the internet. I try to have at least 10 to 15 pieces of reference for each drawing. I then begin to stitch my Frankenstein together, pencilling a line drawing with bits of shading on a sheet of paper. I ink the line drawing and scan it in as line art. Often I will create or complete parts of the drawing in Adobe Illustrator before I move on to colouring. I start colouring in Adobe Photoshop by doing a quick underpainting to work out the tone of the piece. When I am happy with that, I break up the colours into separate layers and begin to render the different parts of the image. Then I begin to merge layers and do group colour adjustments to harmonize the image. Finally, to complete the image, I will make minor colour and lighting adjustments.

illustration
guitar guy

date
2004

media/techniques
adobe photoshop, adobe illustrator

illustration (left)
punk girl

date
2004

media/techniques
adobe photoshop, adobe
illustrator

illustration (right)
finger girl

date
2004

media/techniques
adobe photoshop, adobe
illustrator

illustration (left)
skateboard guy

date
2004

media/techniques
adobe photoshop, adobe
illustrator

illustration (right)
tongue girl

date
2004

media/techniques
adobe photoshop, adobe
illustrator

Gis Castillo

birthplace Aguascalientes, Mexico
education Universidad Autonoma de Aguascalientes, Mexico
inspiration Madonna, Tamara De Lempicka, The Beatles, Coldplay

I grew up in Aguascalientes, Mexico, in a little town where nothing ever changes. While growing up, I was always trying to be different. I expressed myself fearlessly, constantly reinventing myself and creating my own style. At the Universidad Autonoma de Aguascalientes, I studied graphic design, but I have always been drawn to the fashion world. My early work often had a fusion with fashion, but my teachers never approved of these early sketches. However, although they may have been criticized, these illustrations were always controversial, topical and were constantly talked about. That spurred me on to create a personal way to express myself. My main theme is reinvention.

As for my influences, I just love Madonna. I like everything about her: her image, attitude, performances, videos. I am inspired by the world of fashion including, models, designers and photographers. I really admire the painter Tamara De Lempicka and the unique style in which she paints women. There is a real difference in style, fashion and illustration between my native Mexico and the rest of the world. The USA, the UK and France are still the kings of fashion – I discovered that when I was there – and Mexico has little influence on international fashion trends. When I am in Mexico, I keep abreast of international fashion trends through magazines, celebrities and foreign television programmes.

illustration
carolyn fashion icon

date
2003

media/techniques
adobe photoshop,
adobe illustrator

When I start the illustration process, I collect up to 50 fashion pictures to find the perfect pose that I'm looking for, then I draw the figure of the model and make a attractive composition. I produce the vector drawings in Adobe Illustrator and after that I just start to put colour on it. I just work on the composition, colours and textures until I achieve the impact I want and the message I want to send. Usually I just work on the model, but sometimes I also work on the backgrounds at the same time as these are sometimes part of the process.

Most of the time my work is a reflection of my feelings – I am drawn to illustrating women because I feel that fashion, music, pain, love, glamour and women have always been closely linked.

illustration (left)
down

date
2002

media/techniques
adobe photoshop,
adobe illustrator

illustration
lentejuela

date
2003

media/techniques
adobe photoshop,
adobe illustrator

Louis Rodriguez

birthplace Banes, Cuba
education Parsons School of Design, New York City, USA
inspiration Erté, Patrick Nagel, Lillian Baseman, Irving Penn

I was born in the beautiful country of Cuba, land of mambo, Bacardi and cigars. My parents decided to come to the United States, fleeing communism, when I was six and settled in the East Coast. My art interest began to flourish at an early age. Looking back, I remember getting in trouble with my teachers many times because I would be constantly drawing planes, trains and automobiles, and bad renditions of the people inside them, while in class.

The style of my art stems from many things, including, but not limited to, a love of the human body, Art Deco, black-and-white photography, urban and industrial images, and science fiction and fantasy.

My creative thought process sparks off past experiences, present elements that surround me, and visions of the future. Sometimes I find a wealth of inspired ideas in the least expected places. Is there a message behind my illustrations? Maybe, but it's often not intentional. I do find myself using two recurring themes in my illustrations: water, which is natural, life-sustaining, fluid and always moving; and metal, which represents all that is man-made, hard and stable, Art Deco and the age of industry. There is perhaps a social meaning that emerges from my work; but rather than desperately trying to be the next social artist of our times I prefer to create meaning through instinct. Although I am a passionate traditional artist at heart, I have also been working digitally of late. The tools I use range from a simple paintbrush and oil paints to Adobe Photoshop, Corel Painter and a digital camera. I also use Lightwave to generate three-dimensional characters and objects when I need to get the right perspective.

I start out with small roughs, at times barely distinguishable to other viewers, just to note down the idea, composition or flowing gesture. If I really like it, I'll rework it and rework it until it starts taking shape – not losing the original creative thought but rather enhancing it. Next, I'll take digital photos of a live model in poses close to the sketch, always giving creative freedom. I then start painting in Adobe Photoshop, sometimes combining two or three different parts of the photographed poses to make one, to exaggerate and sometimes push the limits of the pose. I continue to paint digitally using different brushes in Adobe Photoshop for varied textural effects until I find a stopping point at which I'm pleased. There are a couple of other approaches I use, but this is the main way I have been working recently. I look forward to the future to watching and experiencing my illustrations evolve and move in new directions.

illustration
pony tail

date
2004

media/techniques
adobe photoshop, corel
painter, lightwave

122

illustration (left)
paris in the waters

date
2004

media/techniques
adobe photoshop, corel
painter, lightwave

illustration
rose

date
2004

media/techniques
adobe photoshop, corel
painter, lightwave

Hiroko Hasegawa

birthplace Tokyo, Japan
education Setsu Mode Seminar, Tokyo, Japan
inspiration Pablo Picasso, Dick Bruna

I was born in Tokyo, Japan. I studied illustration at Setsu Mode Seminar, where I learned traditional methods of painting and drawing.

My main work is creating illustrations for magazines such as *LEE*, *Urb*, *Caz* and *CREA*. I also illustrate book covers, websites and advertisements for companies such as *Shiseido* and Kintetsu Department store. I have also had my own exhibition at the HB Gallery in Tokyo, featuring my unpublished illustrations.

My favourite artists are Pablo Picasso and the children's book illustrator Dick Bruna. There is power in their work and my heart is always moved by it. I try to take a similar approach in my own work. I also love fashion: I get ideas from looking at the clothes in the Paris, London, Milan and Tokyo collections. The colours, form, motion and space are special and influence my illustrations. Also, I love to draw while listening to music; it inspires me.

illustration
sunshine

date
2001

media/techniques
adobe photoshop

I create my illustrations either by hand, using watercolour paper, watercolour and gouache, or with a computer, using Adobe Photoshop. Sometimes I combine both methods. Although I am happy working either way, I probably prefer to draw using traditional methods. I like to feel the watercolour or gouache leading my illustration – it is a good sensation. I sketch both from life and from my imagination. The subject of my illustrations are usually suggested to me by my clients. I develop the theme in my head and I transfer the image that emerges to my hand to give it shape and form.

illustration (right)
sheep year

date
2003

media/techniques
watercolour, watercolour
paper, gouache

illustration (left)
chair

date
2001

media/techniques
watercolour, watercolour
paper, gouache

illustration (left)
blue

date
2002

media/techniques
watercolour, watercolour
paper, gouache

illustration (above)
look up

date
2000

media/techniques
watercolour, watercolour
paper, gouache

133

Seiko Ohmori

birthplace Iwate, Japan
education Musashino Art University, Japan
inspiration Kiitsu Suzuki, Mika Nunagawa, Yosihiko Ueda, Redon Odilon

I was born in Iwate, Japan. I work as a freelance illustrator, creating advertisements for department stores, PR magazines, and book and CD covers. In 2000, I was awarded a bronze medal at the Three-dimensional and Digital Illustration Awards Show, USA, and have received many other prizes. To date, I have had seven solo exhibitions.

I enjoy travel and experiencing the landscapes and cultures of different countries, and am especially attracted by the colour combinations in traditional costumes. Films, nature, the scent of the streets and many other elements combine to give my pieces their form. But I am most interested in what it means to be born a woman. I want to explore the strength, depth, richness and flexibility of being female. This is inevitably reflected in the processes of my work, and my major theme is how to express a woman's inner world. In creating my work, rather than relying on logic and theory, I strive towards developing my intuition to the fullest.

To produce my illustrations I initially draw a rough sketch to decide the figure's angle, the flow of its hair and the way it is shaped before I actually start making it. I then create a three-dimensional model in polymer clay. Usually, I create the clothing part with polymer clay – sometimes mixing with a natural material such as yarn, hemp, string or branches – but I rarely use actual cloth for the costumes, although I have done so on occasion. This is because plaster and cloth have a totally different sense of materials – if they are not used in exactly the right way, the model will be quite unbalanced. I then photograph the models, scan the photographs into a computer and then digitally manipulate the images. I must always be very careful with quantity and colour that are used when I am making the models. As all the three-dimensional works will be printed and, as a result, become two-dimensional, I must always think of the balance, foreseeing the final, photographed work.

illustration
spring wind

date
2001

media/techniques
polymer clay, acrylic, gouache, sand, yarn, cloth

illustration
songstress in autumn

date
2003

media/techniques
gypsum clay, acrylic, gouache,
sand, yarn

illustration
a day that will be wind someday

date
2002

media/techniques
gypsum clay, acrylic, gouache,
sand, yarn, hemp, string

illustration (left)
flower that blows in winter

date
2003

media/techniques
gypsum clay, acrylic, gouache,
sand, yarn

Ling Chen

birthplace Canton, China
education Parsons School of Design, New York City, USA
inspiration Aubrey Beardsley, Leonardo da Vinci, New York City, friends and family

Tell me about yourself
I was born in China, although New York has been my home since I was two. I studied at Parsons School of Design, where I majored in Fashion and then Illustration. I am a freelance artist, sending my fashion illustrations to magazines and to fashion companies.

Why are you attracted to drawing and illustration?
I've always drawn. I think the basis of all art is drawing. It both reveals and conceals and it is this aspect that fascinates me and which I try to explore in my work.

How do you feel about traditional illustration and digital illustration?
There will always be a difference between the two mediums. Digital is part of a never-ending evolution, like photography was to painting in the 19th century. I choose to use the computer because it creates unexpected and infinite possibilities for artists. Digital technology makes fashion illustration accessible to a wider population and easier for people to produce high-quality graphics.

How do you begin an illustration?
Once I am inspired by something I try to develop it into a concept, do some image references, and then start drawing. New York City is always an inspiration. I also use photographs from magazines and my own photographs. I rarely include my initial sketches in the final work, preferring instead to execute my illustrations with my computer in Adobe Illustrator and Macromedia FreeHand.

How do you approach fashion illustration?
I use a completely different approach when creating fashion illustrations. It is possible to create a different kind of reality. You have to be much more sensitive to the figures and the clothes and the illustrations themselves have to convey mood and beauty.

Tell me about the calendar project.
The inspiration for this project was decadence – the decadence of fashion and decadence in the new millennium. I was fascinated by rococo and baroque French furniture during the process. It was never to my taste but I became very interested in that period for this calendar series and I just started layering all these inspirations into the illustrations. Many artists have illustrated the horoscope and it seemed a natural choice for a calendar. I wanted to illustrate a world that is unfamiliar, even uncomfortable, where innocence may still exist.

Do you have any favourite artists or designers?
Aubrey Beardsley is one of my favourite illustrators, and some people have recognized his influence in the calendar series, although I didn't look at his work for inspiration during the process. Leonardo da Vinci is also one of my favourite artists.

illustration
virgo

How do you know when your work is finished?
I don't know. I am constantly working on my illustrations. It is so convenient with digital media to continually change the colours or move objects around – I am constantly recycling my work to make completely different illustrations.

date
2004

media/techniques
adobe illustrator,
macromedia freehand

Is there a message in your work?
I don't see any reason to impose meaning on my work because everybody sees things differently. Why not give others the freedom to interpret what they want to see?

illustration
aries

date
2004

media/techniques
adobe illustrator,
macromedia freehand

illustration
gemini

date
2004

media/techniques
adobe illustrator,
macromedia freehand

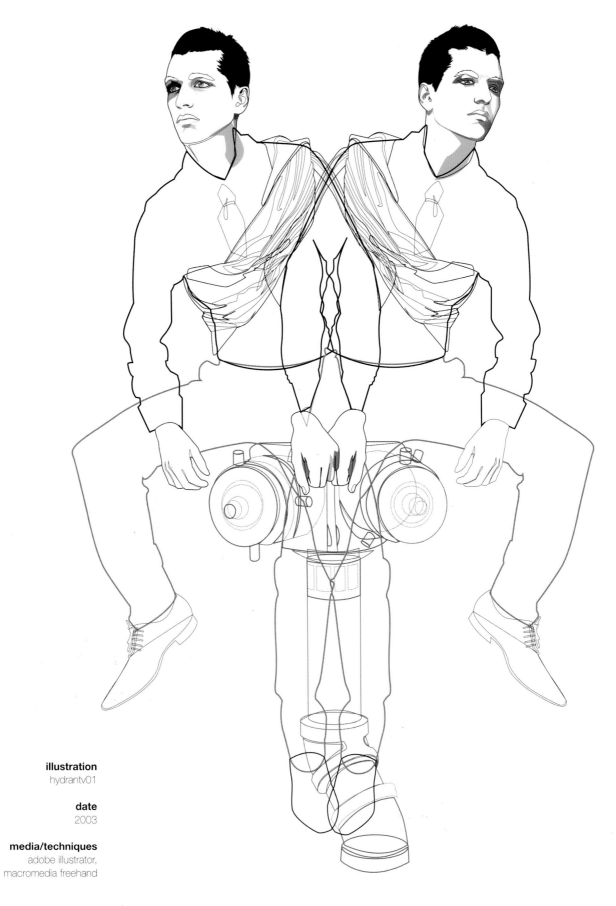

illustration
hydrantv01

date
2003

media/techniques
adobe illustrator,
macromedia freehand

illustration
hydrantv02

date
2003

media/techniques
adobe illustrator,
macromedia freehand

Chul-Yong Choi

birthplace Seoul, Korea
education Hong-Ik University, Seoul, Korea; Domus Academy, Milan, Italy
inspiration Andy Warhol, David Hockney, Antoni Tàpies

I grew up in Seoul, Korea. I graduated in textile art from Hong-Ik University in Seoul, and went on to do further postgraduate study in fashion design and fashion illustration at the same university. After moving to Milan in 2002, I graduated in 2003 with an MA in fashion design from Domus Academy. I am currently based in Milan.

I am now working as a fashion designer at a jeans company called Meltin' Pot. I am also in the process of writing and illustrating a children's book about fashion and shoes. It is an attempt to reinterpret the drawing style of traditional fairy tales, such as *Snow White*, which I recall from my childhood. I am experimenting with texture to make the illustrations look different: spreading acrylic thickly, using dyed gauze for the backgrounds and working with different types of papers and textiles. I have also produced illustrations for the young communications magazine *TTL* and the fashion magazine *LAVICE*. In these, I worked with simple drawings using textured backgrounds and naturally blurred inks.

I am interested in drawing on different papers, fabrics and even things people discarded. I am fascinated by how the other artists have recorded the people and everyday objects of their own era. As Andy Warhol showed 1960s colours and products based on social culture and David Hockney showed peoples' look and interiors from his early 1970s lifestyle, I love to illustrate today's fashion style using the things that are all around me. I am especially attracted to things that have been abandoned: clothes, old bill posters, the faded receipts – these are commonplace and routine, but become my precious inspirations and materials.

In my work, I have always pursued the balance of hand and computer skills. As I have an education in the fine arts and a professional background as a fashion designer and illustrator, I have found the results of hand-drawing alone can be too heavy, where as computer drawings often come out too flat.

illustration
a-line skirt

date
2004

media/techniques
stitching, collage, adobe
photoshop

I usually blend or combine a few materials together: heavy textiles and tweeds, pen and paper, Sumi inks and acrylics, and so on. In this series of illustrations I worked with a collage technique, cutting out the shapes sharply but as naturally as possible. I used many different materials such as linen, suede, leather, lace, and hair. In some cases, these materials were applied directly onto the illustration – otherwise they were reworked in Adobe Photoshop by adjusting colours, changing the scale, or multiplying the layers to create new textures. I also used a sewing machine to stitch the contour of the models onto the fabrics, then scanned them. Finally, in the computer I transformed and duplicated the stitches as necessary.

I redesign, and manipulate my work on the computer, often focusing on a specific part or section of the body, such as from head to chest, or from waist to toe. I have found that this combination of hand-craft and computer work produces interesting results. Because my work constantly surprises me, I am never bored.

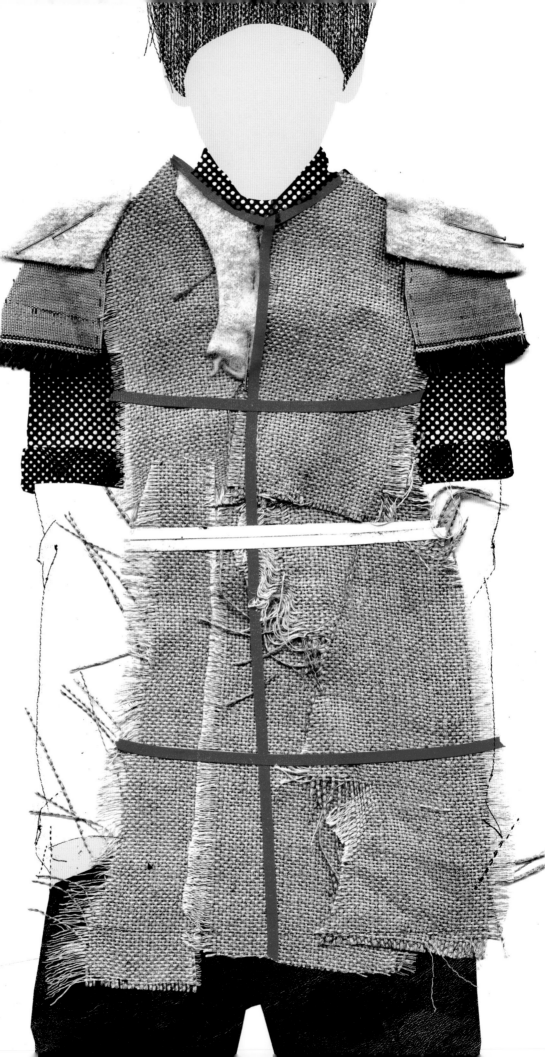

illustration
knight

date
2002

media/techniques
stitching, collage, copypaper,
adobe photoshop

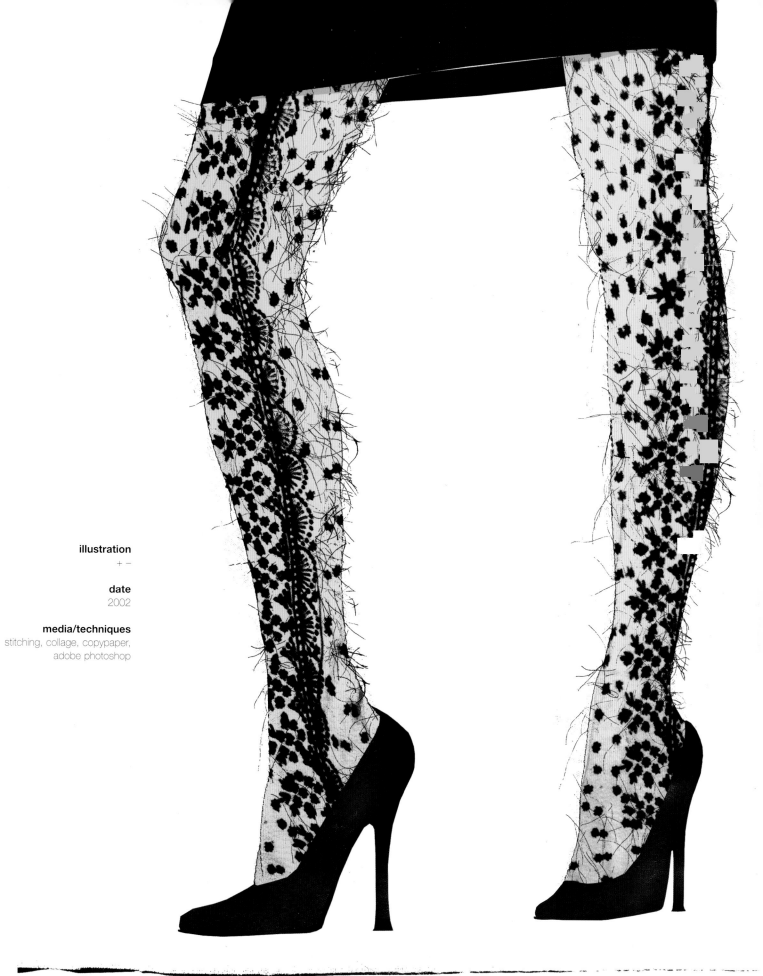

illustration
+ –

date
2002

media/techniques
stitching, collage, copypaper,
adobe photoshop

Hayato Jome

birthplace Akita, Japan
education Musashino Art University, Tokyo, Japan
inspiration Gustav Klimt, Marc Chagall, Tsune Nakamura, Jan Vermeer

I was born in Akita, Japan. Growing up in my parents' home (a hotel that was not in business), my first impressions of art came from an old fusuma painting, which hung in one of the drawing rooms.

At high school I joined the fine arts club, and became more interested in art by the day, often staying in the school building until midnight to continue drawing. My favourite artists at the time were Gustav Klimt, Marc Chagall, Tsune Nakamura, Jan Vermeer and many more. In the end I took an entrance examination for the art school and in 1980 graduated from Musashino Art University, Tokyo, with a major in oil painting.

My earliest work as an illustrator is all in black and white. In 1979, I illustrated an old tennis magazine called *Smash*, and supported myself doing black and white illustrations in this way for ten years or more. My first exhibition was in 1987 at Art Wad's in Tokyo, and it was here that I first explored working with colour. There have been two private exhibitions since then – Seibu Habitat Gallery, Tokyo, in 1988 and Gleeting Square, Tokyo, in 1995 – but I did not arrive at my present style until the Gallery House MAYA exhibition in Tokyo, in 2001. It is here that I realized the value of portrait drawings.

I don't use photographs, but sketch immediately onto a canvas board with acrylic paints. The process consists of two working stages, first drawing outlines on a board that is covered with oil, and, after wiping off the oil, adding colour using Gel medium paints. The unusual texture of the paintings is achieved by applying and blotting acrylic paint until the desired effect is achieved, which can be quite a long process. I draw very quickly when sketching in some outlines, and take my time during the details. One Japanese influence in my work is to suppress colour as much as possible. There are only five colours in my palette now: red, yellow, blue, black and white. I only use cerulean blue and cobalt blue. Once I have completed this process I make it into a digital image using Adobe Photoshop.

illustration
chin-chiku-lin

date
2000

media/techniques
acrylic on canvas paper,
adobe photoshop

For me, fashion takes the form of a fascination with the human shape, so I try to make sure that the dress of the person in my picture is minimized. Although it may be contrary to the word 'fashion', I feel that the most important thing in the illustration process is to express the eternal and unchanging elements of the human body – these elements are apparent in everyone from the teenagers striding along the street to the old man who is retired. In my pictures the versatility of expression is the surely drawn element.

illustration
summer-coloured maya

date
2003

media/techniques
acrylic on canvas paper,
adobe photoshop

illustration
the old letters

date
2002

media/techniques
acrylic on canvas paper,
adobe photoshop

Toko Ohmori

birthplace Yamaguchi-ken, Japan
education Tokyo Zokei University, Tokyo, Japan
inspiration Reiji Matsumoto, Fusako Kuramochi, Gustav Klimt, Aubrey Beardsley

I was born in the Yamaguchi region of Japan and brought up in Tokyo and Chiba district. When I was little, I wanted to become a vet. But I was very much impressed by the works of the Japanese manga (or comic book) artists Reiji Matsumoto and Fusako Kuramochi and went on to study oil and representational painting at Tokyo Zokei University.

My work has been used on publicity posters, direct mail, book covers, websites, leaflets and T-shirts. My clients range from clothes shops to book publishers and include Max Factor, Sony, *ELLE* and Hachette.

People may consider my work to be fashion illustration, but I draw pictures simply because I love to create my own world on paper (or screen), and I particularly like drawing faces and bodies. Artists and designers who have touched my heart include Egon Schiele, for his strong figures, sensitive use of line and expressive faces; Gustav Klimt, for the combination of beautiful textures and the human form; and Friedensreich Hundertwasser, for his fantastic patterned streets.

When I produce my illustrations I first make a sketch based on a photograph or magazine. I usually work digitally, using Adobe Photoshop and Adobe Illustrator software. Working on screen, I add colours, using a mouse as you would a paintbrush in an oil painting, and then erase what I want to erase. Sometimes, I scan in patterns and lines in watercolour and actual textiles and work with them in Adobe Photoshop to produce a mixed media or collage effect.

illustration
autumn 2003

date
2003

media/techniques
collage, adobe illustrator,
adobe photoshop

The difference between fashion illustration and fashion photography is that the medium of illustration allows me to manipulate the images and add emotion to the figures and faces that I draw. The subjects of my illustrations are ethereal women who are stuck between childhood and adulthood. I am trying to capture the transience and mental conflict of growing up. I want people who see my pictures to feel the emotions I seek to convey. My fashion and lifestyle illustrations are a means of expressing my personal feelings.

illustration
thinking of you

date
2003

media/techniques
watercolour, adobe illustrator,
adobe photoshop

illustration (opposite)
autumn 2

date
2004

media/techniques
pencils, adobe photoshop

illustration
thinking of you 1

date
2003

media/techniques
pencil, cloth, adobe photoshop

illustration
autumn 2004

date
2004

media/techniques
photography, adobe photoshop

Index

illustration
flight (detail)

artist
anjin

date
2004

media/techniques
adobe photoshop, corel painter

illustration
goth girl (detail)

artist
anjin

date
2004

media/techniques
adobe photoshop, corel painter

Contact Information

ANJIN
Email: anjin@anjindesign.com
Website: www.anjindesign.com

KATRIN ASSMAN
Email: ak.assmann@web.de
Website: www.illustratoren.de
Tel (Germany): 030 26 36 94 95
Represented by: Die Illustratoren
Tel (Germany): 040 250 40 50

KAI BARDELEBEN
Email: Kai.Bardeleben@web.de
Website: www.illustratoren.de
Tel (Germany): 040 40 48 61
Represented by: Die Illustratoren
Tel (Germany): 040 250 40 50

GIS CASTILLO
Email: gismadonn@hotmail.com
Website: www.gis.ya.st

LING CHEN
Email: maomao78@gmail.com
Tel (USA): 1 646 643 6161

CHUL-YONG CHOI
Email: ciellion@hotmail.com
Tel (Italy): 340 965 8041

JONATHAN DeLAGARDE
Email: jonathan_delagarde@hotmail.com

FRÉDÉRIC DESMOTS
Email: fred.desmots@freesbee.fr
Tel (France): 02 33 27 53 98

FAWN GEHWEILER
Email: fawn@nocandy.org
Website: www.nocandy.org
Tel (USA): 1 323 327 7609

STÉPHANE GODDARD
Email: goddards@noos.fr
Website: www.agent002.com
Tel (France): 06 63 27 67 81

FLO H
Email: illustratorscave@hotmail.com
Tel (UK): 020 85081912

HIROKO HASEGAWA
Email: sheep@suisen.x0.com
Website: www.suisen.sakura.ne.jp/~sheep/

LISA HENDERLING
Email: henderling@aol.com
Website: www.lisahenderling.com
Tel (USA): 1 845 876 8736
Represented by: Shannon Associates
Website: www.shannonassociates.com
Tel (USA): 1 212 333 2551

GIULIO IURISSEVICH
Email: iuri.g@aliceposta.it
Website: www.giulio-iurissevich.com
Tel (Italy): 04 34 36 31 74

TATJANA JEREMIC
Email: info@happyform.com
Website: www.happyform.com
Tel (Sweden): 08 100 201

HAYATO JOME
Email: jome@j.email.ne.jp
Website: www.peacecard.com/jome.html
Tel (Japan): 03 3405 8816

KALANI LEE
Email: aloha@kalanilee.com
Website: www.kalanilee.com
Represented by: Kate Larkworthy Artist
          Representation, LTD
Email: kate@larkworthy.com
Website: www.larkworthy.com

ALBERT MORELL
Email: albertmorell@inter.net
Website: www.albertmorell.com
Tel (Germany): 030 44 04 49 71

PATRICK MORGAN
Email: patrick.morgan@ite-exhibitions.com
Tel (UK): 07957 687 833

SEIKO OHMORI
Email: seiko_426@ybb.ne.jp
Website: www.se.batic2.com

TOKO OHMORI
Email: toko@rocket.ne.jp
Website: www.toko.rocket.ne.jp
Fax (Japan): 03 5614 9518

KAREN OXMAN
Email: k@karenoxman.com
Website: www.karenoxman.com

ANNETTE-MARIE PEARCY
Email: annette@annettemarie-illustrations.co.uk
Website: www.annettemarie-illustrations.co.uk
Tel (UK): 07899 900 363

ERIN PETSON
Email: epetson99@yahoo.com
Tel (UK): 07967 120 127

ROB PHILLIPS
Email: robphilips@hotmail.com
Tel (UK): 07748 526 851

JEN RENNINGER
Email: jenrenninger@mac.com
Website: www.jenrenninger.com
Tel (USA): 1 877 674 7743

SOPHIE ROBERT
Email: sofirobert@hotmail.com
Tel (France): 06 08 28 40 48

LOUIS RODRIGUEZ
Email: ArtbyLouis@msn.com
Website: www.zyworld.com/Louismedia
Tel (USA): 1 719 640 6105

BÉATRICE SAUTEREAU
Email: bsautereau@tiscali.fr
Website: www.agent002.com
Tel (France): 01 44 09 80 88

JEFF SPOKES
Email: j.spokes@shaw.ca
Website: www.spokesillustration.com
Tel (Canada): 1 306 664 6354

AUTUMN WHITEHURST
Email: awhitehurst@acedsl.com
Tel (USA): 1 718 522 7341
Website: altpick.com/members.php?id=11198
Website: www.art-dept.com